The Heart Healthy Cookbook For Beginners 2022

1000 Days of Flavorful Recipes to Boost your Energy and Support Healthy Blood Pressure and Circulation Including 21-Day No Stress Meal Plan

Becca Russell

TABLE OF CONTENTS

TABLE OF CONTENTS

TABLE OF CONTENTS

TABLE OF CONTENTS

TABLE OF CONTENTS

Chapter 7
DESSERTS AND SMOOTHIE RECIPES 111

Chapter 8
21 DAYS MEAL PLAN 124

INTRODUCTION

According to the World Health Organization, cardiovascular disease is the leading cause of death in the United States, accounting for 1 in 4 deaths.

Each year, an estimated 605,000 people in the US have a first myocardial infarction – and about 610,000 have a first stroke.

But there is another fact that is even more disconcerting:

"Every 36 seconds, an American experiences the onset of a heart attack." This, according to data from the *Center for Disease Control and Prevention* (CDC)

These figures are scary, I know.

But the good news for you is that if you make changes to your diet by following the recipes and advice of this recipe book, you will be able to look after the health of your heart, making it stronger and healthier.

In addition, you will find out which foods are good for your heart and which ones are best avoided.

And at the end, you will get 150 tasty recipes for the next to prepare for you and your family for the next 1,000 days.

▌1. What are cardio vascular diseases?

Cardiovascular diseases are a group of disorders of the heart and blood vessels.

Usually, their cause is an accumulation of fat deposits in the arteries (atherosclerosis) or an increase in blood clots.

A person may be symptomatic (physically experiencing the disease) or asymptomatic (not feeling anything).

However, there are different types of cardiovascular disease.

Let's take a look at them:

- **Arrhythmia**: a problem with your heart's electrical conduction system that can lead to abnormal heart rhythms or heart rates
- **Valve disease**: issues with your heart valves
- **Coronary artery disease**: problems with the blood vessels of the heart, such as blockages
- **Heart failure**: problem with the pumping/relaxing functions of the heart, leading to fluid accumulation and shortness of breath
- **Peripheral artery disease**: problems with blood vessels in the arms, legs, or abdominal organs, such as narrowing or obstructions
- **Aortic disease**: problem with the large blood vessel that channels blood from the heart to the brain and the rest of the body, such as dilation or aneurysm
- **Congenital heart disease**: heart problem that you have had since birth and which can affect different parts of the heart
- **Pericardial disease**: problem with the lining of the heart, including pericarditis and pericardial effusion
- **Cerebrovascular diseases**: problems with blood vessels supplying blood to the brain, such as narrowing or blockages
- **Deep vein thrombosis**: a blockage in the veins, the vessels that bring blood back from the brain/body to the heart.

2. The 6 bad habits that hurt your heart

Taking care of your heart is one of the top acts of self-love. By doing so, you are effectively safeguarding your well-being and ensuring better chances of enjoying a long and healthy life.

Since the heart suffers from a wrong lifestyle and harmful habits, it does not really take much to take care of it. Just eliminate such daily habits that in the long run can cause it to suffer, and the results will be better health and a more efficient heart that is functioning properly.

Here are 6 harmful habits that you should get rid of as soon as possible to safeguard the health of your heart.

1. **Smoking**. It is not surprising news that smoking is bad for you. Indeed, smoking cigarettes, cigars, and pipe is as bad for your heart and arteries as well as for your lungs.

If you have a smoking habit, quitting it is the greatest health gift you can give yourself. Secondhand smoke is also toxic, so avoid it whenever possible.

2. **Lack of exercise**. Regular physical activity provides your body with "magic bullets" against heart disease and other chronic conditions.

The American Heart Association recommends a total of 150 minutes of moderate activity (such as walking or moderate strength training) or 75 minutes of vigorous exercise (running) per week.

3. **Obesity**. Carrying extra pounds, especially around your belly, strains your heart and leads to diabetes. If you are overweight, losing even just 5% to 10% of your original weight can make a big difference to blood pressure and blood sugar.
4. **Bad diet**. Add fruits and vegetables, whole grains, unsaturated fats, good protein (from beans, nuts, fish, and poultry), herbs, and spices to your diet.

Avoid processed foods, salt, fast-digesting carbs (from white bread, white rice, potatoes, and the like), red meat, carbonated drinks, or other sugary drinks (more about that soon).

5. **Alcohol**. If you drink alcohol, try to cut your intake: from one to two drinks a day for men, not more than one a day for women.
6. **Stress**. It may occur as exhaustion, depression, headaches, panic attacks, anxiety, insomnia, weight fluctuations, hair loss, and tics. And its symptoms affect both your private and professional life.

A joint study by the Center for Emotional Intelligence and the Child Study Center of the University of Yale and Leipzig, reported by The New York Times, highlighted how one in five workers - about 20% of the total - is at serious risk of burnout.

And I guess you know how extreme stress can be a trigger for a heart attack.

3. 7 practical tips to protect your heart and prevent disease

So, what can I do to keep the risk of disease to a minimum?

Luckily, there are many things you can do to reduce your chances of heart disease.

Some of the tips you will read below may seem elementary and obvious, while some others will seem "strange" if you have never heard of them.

Let's take a look at them:

1. **Get at least 7 hours of sleep**

According to a new study published in Sleep Health magazine, the heart of people who sleep 5 hours or less a night is about 1.5 years older than the heart of those who get 7 hours of proper rest.

"Sleep is so incredibly important, that no matter how well you eat or how much you work out if you don't get enough rest, the benefits of those healthy lifestyles are substantially reduced," says study co-author Julia Durmer, a researcher in medicine and public health at Emory University in Atlanta.

2. **Eat early**

Have you ever heard the saying, "King's breakfast, prince's lunch, and pauper's dinner?"

There, just be aware that a recent study published in the Cell Metabolism journal found that consuming all your daily calories before 3 p.m. can lower your blood pressure by 10 to 11 mmHg in just five weeks.

"It helps your body get rid of excess sodium if you eat at the beginning of the day," says study author Courtney M. Peterson, Ph.D., an assistant professor of Nutrition Science at the University of Alabama.

3. Take a coffee break (or three!)

Coffee has been extensively studied – and the results are remarkably consistent: "Drinking up to three cups a day is associated with a lower risk of developing cardiovascular disease and death from heart disease," says Frank Hu, MD, Ph.D., president of the Department of Nutrition at the Harvard TH Chan School of Public Health.

Why is that? "It's probably the mix of antioxidants, polyphenols, and other compounds," says Dr. Hu.

4. Take a 25-minute music break

Listening to classical music for less than half an hour can dramatically lower your blood pressure and heart rate, according to a study by the Ruhr University of Bochum in Germany. Relaxing and slow-paced melodies appear to lower your cortisol levels, a stress hormone that contributes to hypertension.

What if you don't like classical music?

You can still do it! Researchers say that as long as the music you listen to is without lyrics and you find it enjoyable, it will probably have a positive impact on your heart anyways. Just give it a try and see how it goes.

5. Get up every 30 minutes

A recent Scottish study comparing postmen and office employees found that people who sit for a long time have a larger waistline and an increased risk of heart disease.

So, whether you're a white-collar worker or spend long hours sitting on the couch watching Netflix, get up at least every half an hour.

Do you know why?

Because "After 30 minutes sitting in a chair, some enzymes in the legs become inactive, leading to the accumulation of 'bad' LDL cholesterol over time," says study co-author William Tigbe, Ph.D. Alexa. So, set a reminder to move! It'll do you good.

6. Do you have a four-legged companion?

If you don't, consider getting one.

Single people who have one or more furry friends are 36% less likely to die from cardiovascular disease than those without a dog, notes a recent Swedish study based on more than 3.4 million adults.

"While we have noted a reduced risk in all types of families, singles have shown the greatest cardiac improvements," says Tove Fall, Ph.D., associate professor of epidemiology at the University of Uppsala and the author of the study.

"It's probably connected to the social benefits of owning a dog, like going for walks in the park and having a companion to curl up with."

7. Make some home-cooked food

"No matter how often you go out to eat, try to cut down on it. And that includes everything – from restaurant dining with friends, to stopping at Starbucks for a muffin," says Jessica Crandall Snyder, RDN, owner of Vital RD, where she specializes in modifying people's cardiac diet.

According to statistics from the Center for Science in the Public Interest, most fast-food meals contain more than 1,500 mg of sodium and in some restaurant chains it's not uncommon to find appetizers with 2K, 3K, or even 4K mg – way saltier than the 700 to 800 mg that Crandall Snyder recommends.

▌ 4. 10 foods that are enemies of your heart

What foods should you avoid as much as possible if you want to protect your heart health?

Here is my list:

Fast-food burgers

Science is not entirely clear on whether saturated fats are really linked to heart disease.

When consumed in moderation, beef fed with high-quality grass can also have some benefits for heart health.

Processed meat and cured meats

Cold cuts (such as bacon and sausages) can be high in saturated fats. Six thin slices of cured meat can contain half the recommended daily sodium, according to the American Heart Association.

Deep-fried foods

Several studies have linked the consumption of fried foods – such as French fries, fried chicken, and fried snacks – to an increased risk of heart disease. Conventional

frying methods create trans fats, a type of fat known to increase bad cholesterol and lower the good type.

Candy

For many years, fat has been labeled as the leading dietary cause of heart disease.

But a report published last year in Jama Internal Medicine revealed that studies funded by the sugar industry were largely responsible for promoting such beliefs.

Nowadays, experts agree that diets high in added sugar can pose just as great a threat because they contribute to obesity, inflammation, high cholesterol, and diabetes – all of which are risk factors for heart disease.

Soft drinks and sugary juices

For many Americans, the main source of added sugar in their diet is not food, but beverages. Recent government reports found that between 2011 and 2014, over 60% of children, 54% of adult men, and 45% of adult women drank at least one sweetened drink or soda beverage per day.

Sweetened cereals

Foods that feel like part of a balanced diet, such as breakfast cereals, can also be overloaded with sugar. "Eating refined carbohydrates and sugars in the morning will cause inflammation and cause your blood sugar to spike and plummet, so you'll crave more sugar during the day," says Dr. Regina Druz, associate professor of cardiology at Hofstra University and chief of cardiology at St. John Episcopal Hospital in New York City.

Instead, she recommends having fruit along with an egg or avocado on whole-grain toast.

Cookies and pastries

Most baked goods, especially commercially produced ones, are full of sugar and probably made with saturated fats (like butter or palm oil) or trans fats (such as partially hydrogenated vegetable oil).

Margarine

Trans fats are common in margarine sticks that are solid at room temperature, although they are often marketed as a healthier alternative to butter.

Opt for a soft margarine spread that does not contain partially hydrogenated oils, or – even better! – stick with olive oil instead.

Pizza

After cold cuts and cured meats, pizza comes second on the American Heart Association's list of salty foods. Other "salt bombs" to keep an eye on include soups, condiments, and salad dressings.

The sodium content of pizza, as well as its saturated fats, increases as extra cheese and meat-based toppings are added. When you eat out or order pizza delivery, limit yourself to one or two slices and choose veg toppings.

Diet soda

It may be fat-free and zero-calorie, but there's still a shady side to diet soda. "People think it's healthy, when in fact it isn't," says Dr. Druz.

A growing number of studies links cola to increased risk factors for heart diseases, including obesity and diabetes.

5. 11 foods that are good for your heart

1. Green leafy vegetables

Prioritize eating green leafy vegetables such as spinach, kale, zucchini, arugula, fennel, etc. because they are rich in vitamin K and folates, which helps protect the arteries.

- But not just that! These foods:
- reduce blood pressure
- slow down the aging process of the arteries
- improve the functionality of blood vessel lining

Ideally, you should consume at least 1 serving of vegetables both at lunch and for dinner, and even as a snack, maybe in the form of homemade juice.

2. Fresh and dried fruit

Fresh fruit is rich in vitamins A, B1, B2, B3, and C which protect the heart and arteries.

You should eat oranges and citrus fruits in general, as well as mango, kiwi, plums, apricots, cherries, apples, melon, and pineapple.

Also, eat berries and red fruits (blueberries, raspberries, blackberries, currants, strawberries) that contain antioxidants (substances that can counteract, slow down, or neutralize free radicals) and help keep bad cholesterol and blood pressure under control.

The recommended daily intake is at least 3 servings.

Also excellent are nuts such as walnuts, hazelnuts, and peanuts because they are rich in vitamin E and omega3 fatty acids that fight high blood pressure and "clean" the arteries from bad cholesterol. In this case, the recommended dose is 10-15 grams of dried fruit per day.

3. Fish (especially oily fish)

Oily fish (mackerel and anchovies, for example) and salmon have a high content of omega-3 fatty acids, which reduce the risk of sudden cardiac death, as well as the mortality rate due to heart disease.

It would be beneficial to eat it 3 or 4 times a week.

4. Legumes

Chickpeas, lentils, beans, peas, and broad beans are a source of plant proteins and macronutrients (fiber, carbohydrates) while being low in sugars and fats. In addition, legumes contain essential minerals:

- iron, which lowers bad cholesterol
- potassium, which lowers blood pressure
- phosphorus, which promotes the proper functioning of the muscles, including the heart.

Ideally, they should feature in your diet 2 or 3 times a week.

5. Soybean

Soy is a legume with high protein content. It is also rich in omega 3 fatty acids which, as already mentioned, fight cardiovascular diseases, but also in lecithin, famously rich in phosphorus with anti-cholesterolemic properties.

Soy is therefore capable of maintaining the blood triglycerides low and keeping diabetes – another cardiovascular risk factor – under control.

The recommended dose is 1 serving per day, such as a cup of soy milk or soy yogurt, or 100g of tofu.

6. Cereals (preferably wholegrain)

Bread, whole grain pasta and rice, oats, rye, barley, buckwheat, and quinoa are all rich in fiber and can help reduce bad cholesterol. However, it's important to rotate your choice of cereals, opt for whole grains, and consume a small daily portion (about 70 grams).

7. Coffee and tea (in moderation)

Coffee and tea contain polyphenols – substances with antioxidant and anti-inflammatory properties that can also regulate the metabolism of lipids and glucose. They also keep cholesterol levels at bay and protect the cardiovascular system.

However, it is imperative not to exceed a maximum of 4 to 5 cups of coffee/tea per day.

8. Red wine, in moderation

Red wine is rich in resveratrol, a substance

found in the skin of grapes, especially black varieties. It has antioxidant properties and is capable of counteracting bad cholesterol while boosting the levels of good cholesterol.

Several studies show that consuming 1 glass of red wine a day is beneficial for both the heart and the brain, decreasing the risk of heart attack and stroke.

9. Chocolate (preferably dark chocolate)

Chocolate is a source of flavonoids – a subcategory of polyphenols – which promote the elasticity of blood vessels and reduce the risk of weight gain, with its harmful consequences on cardiovascular health.

Just make sure, however, that it's dark (at least 70% cocoa) and that your daily intake doesn't exceed 10 grams (a small square).

10. Vegetable oils and fats

To season your dishes, opt for extra virgin olive oil that contains oleic acid, a mono-unsaturated fat with protective effects on cardiovascular diseases.

Conversely, animal fats such as butter and lard, or vegetable oils such as palm oil, sauces, and condiments with high-fat content, should be limited.

11. Apple vinegar

Recent studies show that the consumption of apple cider vinegar, alone or in food, seems to have a beneficial effect on the health of the cardiovascular system.

This is because it contains minerals such as phosphorus, sulfur, iron, magnesium, and especially calcium – crucial to strengthen the heart and the body's immune defenses – as well as potassium, which affects the proper functioning of the heart and muscles.

It is also a source of pectin, a water-soluble fiber that can protect your cells and blood vessels, reduce the cholesterol level in the blood, promote a sense of satiety, and hinder the absorption of fats.

CONCLUSION: 1000 DAYS OF HEALTHY FOOD

In this introductory section we have seen what cardiovascular diseases are, the habits to avoid, and my recommendations to safeguard the health of your heart, plus what to put on your dining table and what to remove from your shopping list.

You are ready to start cooking!

It is time to discover the 150 delicious recipes that I have chosen for you.

Don't worry, there are plenty of treats to enjoy and they will all make you feel satisfied and well.

Thanks to these recipes, you can combine different options and enjoy a different menu every day, for more than 1,000 days.

Wondering how that's possible?

Most people have breakfast and two main meals a day.

The choice is up to you of course, but let's take that as an example, even keeping it more simple by assuming you have a routine same breakfast each day.

I have given you 24 fish & seafood dishes, 18 legumes, and in the vegetarian and salads sections you will find 10 recipes that are designed to be a meal in itself. That's 52 options to choose from for one of your main meals.

I have also given you 49 beef and poultry dishes, and 8 pasta recipes. That's 57 options for your second main meal.

If you went through the recipes one by one choosing from the sections in that way, it is an incredible 2965 days before you will get the same combination twice!

It's really that easy to give yourself an interesting healthy and varied diet.

And I also have given you plenty of side dishes that you can combine with your other recipe choices. The possibilities really are endless!

Now, all you have to do is unleash your creativity with the recipes I've prepared for you, and start enjoying your heart-healthy meals.

NOTE: I decided to include some dessert recipes in this book because we all need a treat every once in a while!

However please remember that in a strict low calories regime you have to consume desserts ONLY as a special treat, say, on special occasions. I would suggest once or twice a month is reasonable but if you have any health concerns remember to get advice from your doctor.

SALMON WRAP

15 minutes

0 minutes

1

INGREDIENTS

- 2 oz. low-salt Smoked Salmon
- 2 teaspoon low-fat cream cheese
- ½ medium-size red onion, finely sliced
- ½ teaspoon fresh basil or dried basil
- Pinch of pepper
- Arugula leaves, ½ cup
- 1 Homemade wrap or any whole-meal tortilla

DIRECTIONS

1. Heat the wrap or tortilla in a heated pan or oven. Combine cream cheese, basil, pepper, and spread on the tortilla. Top with salmon, arugula, and sliced onion. Roll up and slice. Serve and enjoy!

NUTRITION

Calories per serving: 285; Carbohydrates: 30g; Protein: 20g; Fats: 12g

FLOUNDER WITH TOMATOES AND BASIL

15 minutes

20 minutes

4

INGREDIENTS

- 1-pound cherry tomatoes
- 4 garlic cloves, sliced
- 2 tablespoons extra-virgin olive oil
- 2 tablespoons lemon juice
- 2 tablespoons basil, cut into ribbons
- ½ teaspoon kosher salt
- ¼ teaspoon freshly ground black pepper
- 4 (5- to 6-ounce) flounder fillets

DIRECTIONS

1. Preheat the oven to 425°F.
2. Mix the tomatoes, garlic, olive oil, lemon juice, basil, salt, and black pepper in a baking dish. Bake for 5 minutes.
3. Remove, then arrange the flounder on top of the tomato mixture. Bake until the fish is opaque and begins to flake, about 10 to 15 minutes, depending on thickness.

NUTRITION

Calories per serving: 73; Fats: 4g; Carbohydrates: 5g; Protein: 7g

GRILLED MAHI-MAHI WITH ARTICHOKE CAPONATA

INGREDIENTS

- 2 tablespoons extra-virgin olive oil
- 2 celery stalks, diced
- 1 onion, diced
- 2 garlic cloves, minced
- ½ cup cherry tomatoes, chopped
- ¼ cup white wine
- 2 tablespoons white wine vinegar
- 1 can artichoke hearts, drained and chopped
- ¼ cup green olives, pitted and chopped
- ¼ teaspoon red pepper flakes
- 2 tablespoons fresh basil, chopped
- 4 (5- to 6-ounces each) skinless mahi-mahi fillets
- ½ teaspoon kosher salt
- ¼ teaspoon freshly ground black pepper
- Olive oil cooking spray

DIRECTIONS

1. Heat olive oil in a skillet over a medium heat, then add the celery and onion, and sauté for 4 to 5 minutes.
2. Add the garlic and sauté for 30 seconds. Add the tomatoes and cook for 2 to 3 minutes.
3. Add the wine and vinegar to deglaze the pan, increasing the heat to medium-high.
4. Add the artichokes, olives, and red pepper flakes and simmer, reducing the liquid by half, for about 10 minutes. Mix in the basil.
5. Season the mahi-mahi with salt and pepper. Heat a grill skillet or grill pan over medium-high heat and coat with olive oil cooking spray. Add the fish and cook for 4 to 5 minutes per side. Serve topped with the artichoke caponata.

15 minutes

30 minutes

4

NUTRITION

Calories per serving: 127; Fats: 4g; Carbohydrates: 9g; Protein: 11g

COD AND CAULIFLOWER CHOWDER

INGREDIENTS

- 2 tablespoons extra-virgin olive oil
- 1 leek, sliced thinly
- 4 garlic cloves, sliced
- 1 medium head of cauliflower, coarsely chopped
- ¼ teaspoon freshly ground black pepper
- 2 cup cherry tomatoes
- 1 cup no-salt-added vegetable stock
- ¼ cup green olives, pitted and chopped
- 1 to 1½ pounds cod
- ¼ cup fresh parsley, minced

DIRECTIONS

1. Heat the olive oil in a Dutch oven or large pot over medium heat. Add the leek and sauté until lightly golden brown, about 5 minutes.
2. Add the garlic and sauté for 30 seconds. Add the cauliflower and black pepper and sauté for 2 to 3 minutes.
3. Add the tomatoes and vegetable stock, increase the heat to high and boil then turn the heat to low and simmer for 10 minutes.
4. Add the olives and mix. Add the fish, cover, and simmer 20 minutes or until fish is opaque and flakes easily. Gently mix in the parsley.

15 minutes

40 minutes

4

NUTRITION

Calories per serving: 172; Fats: 5g; Carbohydrates: 13g; Protein: 18g

SARDINE BRUSCHETTA WITH FENNEL AND LEMON CREMA

15 minutes

0 minutes

4

INGREDIENTS

- 1/3 cup plain Greek yogurt
- 2 tablespoons mayonnaise
- 2 tablespoons lemon juice
- 2 teaspoons lemon zest
- A pinch of salt
- 1 fennel bulb, cored and thinly sliced
- ¼ cup parsley, chopped, plus more for garnish
- ¼ cup of fresh mint, chopped
- 2 teaspoons extra-virgin olive oil
- 1/8 teaspoon freshly ground black pepper
- 8 slices multigrain bread, toasted
- 2 (4.4-ounce) cans of smoked sardines

DIRECTIONS

1. Mix the yogurt, mayonnaise, 1 tablespoon of the lemon juice, the lemon zest, and ¼ teaspoon of the salt in a small bowl.
2. Mix the remaining ½ teaspoon of salt, the remaining 1 tablespoon of lemon juice, the fennel, parsley, mint, olive oil, and black pepper in a separate small bowl.
3. Spoon 1 tablespoon of the yogurt mixture on each piece of toast. Divide the fennel mixture evenly on top of the yogurt mixture. Divide the sardines between the toasts, placing them on top of the fennel mixture. Garnish with more herbs, if desired.

NUTRITION

Calories per serving: 241; Fats: 8g; Carbohydrates: 25g; Protein: 17g

CHOPPED TUNA SALAD

15 minutes

0 minutes

4

INGREDIENTS

- 2 tablespoons extra-virgin olive oil
- 2 tablespoons lemon juice
- 2 teaspoons Dijon mustard
- ¼ teaspoon freshly ground black pepper
- 12 olives, pitted and chopped
- ½ cup celery, diced
- ½ cup red onion, diced
- ½ cup red bell pepper, diced
- ½ cup fresh parsley, chopped
- 2 (6-ounce) cans no-salt-added tuna packed in water, drained
- 6 cups baby spinach

DIRECTIONS

1. Mix the olive oil, lemon juice, mustard, and black pepper in a medium bowl. Add in the olives, celery, onion, bell pepper, and parsley and mix well. Add the tuna and gently incorporate. Divide the spinach evenly between 4 plates or bowls. Spoon the tuna salad evenly on top of the spinach.

NUTRITION

Calories per serving: 146; Fats: 11g; Carbohydrates: 5g; Protein: 9g

MONKFISH WITH SAUTÉED LEEKS, FENNEL, AND TOMATOES

INGREDIENTS

- 1 to 1½ pounds monkfish
- 3 tablespoons lemon juice,
- 1/8 teaspoon freshly ground black pepper
- 2 tablespoons extra-virgin olive oil
- 1 leek, sliced in half lengthwise and thinly sliced
- ½ onion, julienned
- 3 garlic cloves, minced
- 2 bulbs fennel, cored and thinly sliced, plus ¼ cup fronds for garnish
- 1 (14.5-ounce) can no-salt-added diced tomatoes
- 2 tablespoons fresh parsley, chopped
- 2 tablespoons fresh oregano, chopped
- ¼ teaspoon red pepper flakes

DIRECTIONS

1. Place the fish in a medium baking dish and add 2 tablespoons of the lemon juice and the black pepper. Place in the refrigerator.
2. Heat olive oil in a large skillet over medium heat, then put the leek and onion and sauté until translucent, about 3 minutes. Add the garlic and sauté for 30 seconds. Add the fennel and sauté for 4 to 5 minutes. Add the tomatoes and simmer for 2 to 3 minutes.
3. Stir in the parsley, oregano, red pepper flakes, the remaining ¾ teaspoon salt, and the remaining 1 tablespoon of lemon juice. Put the fish on the leek mixture, cover, and simmer for 20 to 25 minutes. Garnish with the fennel fronds.

15 minutes

35 minutes

4

NUTRITION

Calories per serving: 114; Fats: 3g; Carbohydrates: 19g; Protein: 5g

CARAMELIZED FENNEL AND SARDINES WITH PENNE

INGREDIENTS

- 8 ounces whole-wheat penne
- 2 tablespoons extra-virgin olive oil
- 1 bulb fennel, cored and thinly sliced, plus ¼ cup fronds
- 2 celery stalks, thinly sliced, plus ½ cup leaves
- 4 garlic cloves, sliced
- ¼ teaspoon freshly ground black pepper
- Zest of 1 lemon
- Juice of 1 lemon
- 2 (4.4-ounce) cans boneless/skinless sardines packed in olive oil, undrained

DIRECTIONS

1. Cook the penne, as stated on the packaging. Drain, reserving 1 cup of pasta water. Heat olive oil in a large skillet over medium heat, then add the fennel and celery and cook for 10 to 12 minutes. Add the garlic and cook for 1 minute.
2. Add the penne, reserved pasta water and black pepper. Adjust the heat to medium-high and cook for 1 to 2 minutes.
3. Remove, then stir in the lemon zest, lemon juice, fennel fronds, and celery leaves. Break the sardines into bite-size pieces and gently mix in, along with the oil they were packed in.

15 minutes

30 minutes

4

NUTRITION

Calories per serving: 162; Fats: 7g; Carbohydrates: 14g; Protein: 11g

GREEN GODDESS CRAB SALAD WITH ENDIVE

15 minutes

10 minutes

4

INGREDIENTS

- ½ pound lump crabmeat
- 2/3 cup plain Greek yogurt
- 3 tablespoons mayonnaise
- 3 tablespoons fresh chives, chopped, plus extra for garnish
- 3 tablespoons fresh parsley, chopped, plus extra for garnish
- 3 tablespoons fresh basil, chopped, plus extra for garnish
- Zest of 1 lemon
- Juice of 1 lemon
- ¼ teaspoon freshly ground black pepper
- 4 endives, ends cut off and leaves separated

DIRECTIONS

1. In a medium bowl, combine the crab, yogurt, mayonnaise, chives, parsley, basil, lemon zest, lemon juice, salt, plus black pepper and mix until well combined.
2. Place the endive leaves on 4 salad plates. Divide the crab mixture evenly on top of the endive. Garnish with additional herbs, if desired.

NUTRITION

Calories per serving: 154; Fats: 4g; Carbohydrates: 5g; Protein: 22g

SEARED SCALLOPS WITH BLOOD ORANGE GLAZE

INGREDIENTS

- 3 tablespoons extra-virgin olive oil,
- 3 garlic cloves, minced
- 4 blood oranges, juiced
- 1 teaspoon blood orange zest
- ½ teaspoon red pepper flakes
- 1-pound scallops, small side muscle removed
- ¼ teaspoon freshly ground black pepper
- ¼ cup fresh chives, chopped

DIRECTIONS

1. Heat 1 tablespoon of the olive oil in a small saucepan over medium-high heat. Add the garlic and ¼ teaspoon of the salt and sauté for 30 seconds.
2. Add the orange juice and zest, bring to a boil, reduce the heat to medium-low, and cook for 20 minutes, or until the liquid reduces by half and becomes a thicker syrup consistency. Remove and mix in the red pepper flakes.
3. Pat the scallops dry with a paper towel and season with the remaining ¼ teaspoon salt and the black pepper. Heat the remaining 2 tablespoons of olive oil in a large skillet on medium-high heat. Add the scallops gently and sear.
4. Cook on each side for 2 minutes. If cooking in 2 batches, use 1 tablespoon of oil per batch. Serve the scallops with the blood orange glaze and garnish with the chives.

15 minutes

20 minutes

4

NUTRITION

Calories per serving: 300; Fats: 10g; Carbohydrates: 30g; Protein: 33g

LEMON GARLIC SHRIMP

15 minutes

10 minutes

4

INGREDIENTS

- 2 tablespoons extra-virgin olive oil
- 3 garlic cloves, sliced
- ¼ teaspoon red pepper flakes
- 1-pound large shrimp, peeled and deveined
- ½ cup white wine
- 3 tablespoons fresh parsley, finely chopped
- Zest of ½ lemon
- Juice of ½ lemon

DIRECTIONS

1. Heat the olive oil in a wok or large skillet over medium-high heat. Add the garlic, salt, and red pepper flakes and sauté until the garlic starts to brown, 30 seconds to 1 minute.
2. Add the shrimp and cook for 2 to 3 minutes on each side. Pour in the wine and deglaze the wok, scraping up any flavorful brown bits, for 1 to 2 minutes. Turn off the heat; mix in the parsley, lemon zest, and lemon juice.

NUTRITION

Calories per serving: 177; Fats: 5g; Carbohydrates: 1.5g; Protein: 28g

LEMON SALMON WITH KAFFIR LIME

15 minutes

30 minutes

1

INGREDIENTS

- A whole side of salmon fillet
- 1 thinly sliced lemon
- 2 kaffir torn lime leaves
- 1 quartered and bruised lemongrass stalk
- 1 ½ cups fresh coriander leaves

DIRECTIONS

1. Heat oven to 350 F. Cover a baking pan with foil sheets, overlapping the sides (enough to fold over the fish).
2. Put the salmon on the foil, top with the lemon, lime leaves, lemongrass, and 1 cup of the coriander leaves. Option: season with salt and pepper.
3. Bring the long side of the foil to the center before folding to seal. Roll the ends to wrap up the salmon. Bake for 30 minutes. Transfer the cooked fish to a platter. Top with fresh coriander. Serve with white or brown rice.

NUTRITION

Calories per serving: 276; Protein: 24g; Carbohydrates: 12g; Fats: 17g

BAKED FISH SERVED WITH VEGETABLES

INGREDIENTS

- 4 haddock or cod fillets, skinless
- 2 Zucchinis, sliced into thick pieces
- 2 red onions, sliced into thick pieces
- 3 large tomatoes, cut into wedges
- ¼ cup black olives pitted
- ¼ cup flavorless oil (olive, canola, or sunflower)
- 1 tablespoon lemon juice
- 1 tablespoon Dijon mustard
- 2 garlic cloves, minced
- ½ cup chopped parsley

DIRECTIONS

1. Heat oven to 400 F. In a large baking dish, drizzle some oil over the bottom. Place the fish in the middle. Surround the fish with the zucchini, tomato, onion, and olives. Drizzle more oil over the vegetables and fish. Season with salt and pepper.
2. Place the baking dish in the oven. Bake for 30 minutes, or until the fish is flaky and vegetables are tender. In another bowl, whisk the lemon juice, garlic, mustard, and remaining oil. Set aside.
3. Split the cooked vegetables between plates, then top with the fish. Drizzle the dressing over the vegetables and fish. Garnish with parsley.

15 minutes

30 minutes

4

NUTRITION

Calories per serving: 195; Protein: 23g; Carbohydrates:14g; Fats: 6g

FISH IN A VEGETABLE PATCH

INGREDIENTS

- 1-pound halibut fillet, skinless
- 1 tablespoon flavorless oil (olive, canola, or sunflower)
- 1 cup tomato sauce
- 1 ½ tablespoons Worcestershire sauce
- 2 large lemons, juiced
- 1 celery stick, diced
- ½ green pepper, chopped
- 1 large carrot, diced
- ½ onion, diced
- 1/4 lemon, sliced

DIRECTIONS

1. Heat oven to 400 F. In a small saucepan, combine the tomato sauce, Worcestershire sauce, and lemon juice. Heat for 5 minutes.
2. Drizzle oil in a shallow baking dish. Arrange the vegetables along the bottom and lay the fish over the vegetables. Pour the sauce over the fish. Cover with foil.
3. Bake fillet for 15 minutes, or until the fish is cooked and flaky. Dish out the vegetables, place the fish over the top. Garnish the fish with the lemon slices. Serve with white or brown rice.

15 minutes

20 minutes

3

NUTRITION

Calories per serving: 285; Protein: 33g ; Carbohydrates: 16g ; Fats: 9g

15

15 minutes

30 minutes

4

SPICY COD

INGREDIENTS

- 1 pound cod fillets
- 1 tablespoon flavorless oil (olive, canola, or sunflower)
- 1 cup low sodium salsa
- 2 tablespoons fresh chopped parsley

DIRECTIONS

1. Heat oven to 350 F. Drizzle the oil along the bottom of a large, deep baking dish. Place the cod fillets in the dish. Pour the salsa over the fish.
2. Cover with foil for 20 minutes. Remove the foil for the last 10 minutes of cooking. Bake in the oven for 20 – 30 minutes, until the fish is flaky. Serve with white or brown rice. Garnish with parsley.

NUTRITION

Calories per serving: 135; Protein: 20g; Carbohydrates :2.5g; Fats: 4.5g

EASY SHRIMP

INGREDIENTS

- 1-pound cooked shrimp
- 1 pack mixed frozen vegetables (0,5 oz)
- 1 garlic clove, minced
- 1 teaspoon butter or margarine
- ¼ cup of water
- 1 pack of shrimp-flavored instant noodles
- ½ teaspoon ground ginger

DIRECTIONS

1. In a large skillet, melt the butter. Add the minced garlic and sweat it for 1 minute. Add the shrimp and vegetables to the skillet. Season with salt and pepper. Cover and simmer for 5 - 10 minutes, until the shrimp turns pink and the vegetables are tender.
2. Boil water in a separate pot. Add the noodles. Turn off the heat, cover the pot. Let it stand for 3 minutes. (Retain the water.)
3. Using a scoop or tongs, transfer the noodles to the skillet with the shrimp and vegetables. Stir in the seasoning packet. Mix, then serve immediately.

15 minutes

10 minutes

4

NUTRITION

Calories per serving: 198 ; Protein: 30g ; Carbohydrates: 11g ; Fats: 4g

---

STEAMED BLUE CRABS

INGREDIENTS

- 30 live blue crabs
- ½ cup seafood seasoning
- ¼ cup of salt
- 3 cups beer
- 3 cups distilled white vinegar

DIRECTIONS

1. In a large stockpot, combine the seasoning, salt, beer, and white vinegar. Bring to a boil. Put each crab upside down, then stick a knife into the shell just before cooking them. Cover the lid, leaving a crack for the steam to vent.
2. Steam the crabs until they turn bright orange and float to the top. Allow them to cook for another 2 - 3 minutes. Serve immediately.

15 minutes

10 minutes

6

NUTRITION

Calories per serving: 879 ; Protein: 119g ; Carbohydrates: 48g ; Fats: 8g

15 minutes

5 minutes

2

GINGER SESAME SALMON

INGREDIENTS

- 4 ounces salmon
- 1/8 cup low-sodium soy sauce
- 2 tablespoons of balsamic vinegar
- ½ teaspoon sesame oil
- 2-inch chunk ginger, peeled and grated
- 1 garlic clove, minced
- 1 teaspoon flavorless oil (olive, canola, or sunflower)
- 1 teaspoon sesame seeds
- 1 teaspoon green onion, minced

DIRECTIONS

1. In a glass dish, combine the soy sauce, balsamic vinegar, sesame oil, garlic, and ginger. Place the salmon in the dish. Cover and marinate for 15 - 60 minutes in the fridge.
2. In a nonstick skillet, heat 1 teaspoon of oil. Sauté the fish until it becomes firm and golden on each side. Sprinkle the sesame seeds in the pan. Heat for 1 minute. Serve immediately. Garnish with green onion.

NUTRITION

Calories per serving: 218; Protein: 17g ; Carbohydrates: 6.5g ; Fats: 13.5g

STEAMED VEGGIE AND LEMON PEPPER SALMON

INGREDIENTS

- 1 carrot, peeled and julienned
- 1 red bell pepper, julienned
- 1 zucchini, julienned
- ½ lemon, sliced thinly
- 1 tsp pepper
- ½ tsp salt
- 1/2-lb salmon filet with skin on
- A dash of tarragon

DIRECTIONS

1. In a heat-proof dish that fits inside a saucepan, add salmon with skin side down. Season with pepper. Add slices of lemon on top.
2. Place the julienned vegetables on top of the salmon and season with tarragon. Cover the top of the fish with the remaining cherry tomatoes and place the dish on the trivet. Cover the dish with foil. Cover the pan and steam for 15 minutes. Serve and enjoy.

15 minutes

15 minutes

4

NUTRITION

Calories per serving: 125; Carbohydrates: 7g; Protein: 17g; Fats: 3g

STEAMED FISH WITH SCALLIONS AND GINGER

INGREDIENTS

- ¼ cup chopped cilantro
- ¼ cup julienned scallions
- 2 tbsp julienned ginger
- 1 tbsp peanut oil
- 1-lb Tilapia filets
- 1 tsp garlic
- 1 tsp minced ginger
- 2 tbsp rice wine

DIRECTIONS

1. Mix garlic, minced ginger, rice wine, and soy sauce in a heat-proof dish that fits inside a saucepan. Add the Tilapia filet and marinate for half an hour, turning half way through.
2. Cover the dish with foil and place on a trivet. Cover the pan and steam for 15 minutes. Serve and enjoy.

15 minutes

15 minutes

3

NUTRITION

Calories per serving: 181; Carbohydrates: 1.5g; Protein: 27g; Fats: 7g

GARLIC AND TOMATOES ON MUSSELS

15 minutes

15 minutes

6

INGREDIENTS

- ¼ cup white wine
- ½ cup of water
- 3 Roma tomatoes, chopped
- 2 cloves of garlic, minced
- 1 bay leaf
- 1 pound of mussels, scrubbed
- ½ cup fresh parsley, chopped
- 1 tbsp oil
- Pepper

DIRECTIONS

1. Heat a pot on medium-high heat for 3 minutes. Add oil and stir around to coat the pot with oil. Sauté the garlic, bay leaf, and tomatoes for 5 minutes.
2. Add the remaining ingredients except for parsley and mussels. Mix well. Add mussels. Cover, and boil for 5 minutes. Serve with a sprinkle of parsley and discard any unopened mussels.

NUTRITION

Calories per serving: 100; Carbohydrates: 3g; Protein: 4.6g; Fats: 3g

CREAMY HADDOCK WITH KALE

15 minutes

10 minutes

5

INGREDIENTS

- 1 tbsp olive oil
- 1 onion, chopped
- 2 cloves of garlic, minced
- 2 cups of chicken broth
- 1 teaspoon of crushed red pepper flakes
- 1-pound wild Haddock fillets
- 3 tbsp thick cream
- 1 tablespoon basil
- 1 cup kale leaves, chopped
- Pepper to taste

DIRECTIONS

1. Place a pot on medium-high heat for 3 minutes. Add oil, then sauté the onion and garlic for 5 minutes. Add the rest of the ingredients, except for the basil, and mix well. Simmer on low heat for 5 minutes. Serve with a sprinkle of basil.

NUTRITION

Calories per serving: 183; Carbohydrates: 4g; Protein: 15g; Fats: 12g

COCONUT CURRY SEA BASS

INGREDIENTS

- 1 can of coconut milk
- Juice of 1 lime, freshly squeezed
- 1 tablespoon red curry paste
- 1 teaspoon coconut aminos
- 1 teaspoon of honey
- 2 teaspoons sriracha
- 2 cloves of garlic, minced
- 1 teaspoon ground turmeric
- 1 tablespoon curry powder
- ¼ cup fresh cilantro
- Pepper

DIRECTIONS

1. Place a heavy-bottomed pot on medium-high heat. Mix in all the ingredients then simmer on a low heat for 5 minutes. Serve and enjoy.

15 minutes

15 minutes

3

NUTRITION

Calories per serving: 55; Carbohydrates: 7g; Protein: 1g; Fats: 3g

STEWED COD FILET WITH TOMATOES

INGREDIENTS

- 1 tbsp olive oil
- 1 onion, sliced
- 1 ½ pound fresh cod filets
- Pepper
- 1 lemon juice, freshly squeezed
- 1 can diced tomatoes

DIRECTIONS

1. Sauté the onion for 2 minutes in a pot on medium-high heat.
2. Stir in diced tomatoes and cook for 5 minutes.
3. Add the cod filet and season with pepper.
4. Simmer on a low heat for 5 minutes. Serve with freshly squeezed lemon juice.

15 minutes

15 minutes

6

NUTRITION

Calories per serving: 93; Carbohydrates: 3.5g; Protein: 14.5g; Fats: 2.5g

25

DECENT BEEF AND ONION STEW

INGREDIENTS

- 1 pound of lean beef, cubed
- 2 pounds shallots, peeled
- 5 garlic cloves, peeled, whole
- 3 tablespoons tomato paste
- 1 bay leaves
- ¼ cup olive oil
- 3 tablespoons lemon juice

DIRECTIONS

1. Take a stew pot and place it over a medium heat.
2. Add olive oil and let it heat.
3. Add meat and brown.
4. Add the remaining ingredients and cover with water.
5. Bring the whole mix to a boil.
6. Reduce the heat to low and cover the pot.
7. Simmer for 1,5 hours until the beef is cooked thoroughly.
8. Serve hot!

NUTRITION

Calories per serving: 460 ; Fats: 22g; Carbohydrates: 40g; Protein: 30g

10 minutes

1,5 hours

4

26

BEEF SOUP

INGREDIENTS

- 1 pound ground beef, lean
- 1 cup of mixed vegetables, frozen
- 1 yellow onion, chopped
- 6 cups vegetable broth
- 1/2 cup reduced-fat cream
- Pepper to taste

DIRECTIONS

1. Take a stockpot and add all the ingredients except for the cream, salt, and black pepper.
2. Bring to a boil.
3. Reduce the heat to simmer.
4. Cook for 40 minutes.
5. Once cooked, heat the cream.
6. Add the cream once the soup is cooked.
7. Blend the soup till smooth by using an immersion blender.
8. Season with salt and black pepper.
9. Serve and enjoy!

NUTRITION

Calories per serving: 322; Fats: 11g; Carbohydrates: 15g; Protein: 31g

10 minutes

40 minutes

4

BEEF WITH MUSHROOM AND BROCCOLI

INGREDIENTS

For the Beef Marinade:

- 1 garlic clove, minced
- 1 piece of fresh ginger, minced
- Salt and freshly ground black pepper
- 3 tablespoons of white wine vinegar
- 3/4 cup beef broth
- 1 pound flank steak, trimmed and sliced into thin strips

For Vegetables:

- 2 tablespoons coconut oil
- 2 garlic cloves
- 3 cups broccoli rabe
- 4 ounces shiitake mushrooms
- 8 ounces cremini mushrooms

DIRECTIONS

For the marinade:

1. In a substantial bowl, mix all the ingredients except for the beef. Add the beef to the bowl and coat with the marinade generously. Refrigerate for around 1/4 hour.
2. In a substantial skillet, heat the oil on a medium-high heat.
3. Remove the beef from the bowl, reserving the marinade.
4. Put the the beef and garlic in the skillet and cook for about 3-4 minutes or till browned.
5. In the same skillet, add the reserved marinade, broccoli and mushrooms. Cook for approximately 3-4 minutes.
6. Give the mixture around the beef a quick stir and then cook for about 3-4 more minutes.

60 minutes

12 minutes

4

NUTRITION

Calories per serving: 125; Carbohydrates: 17g; Fats: 6.5g; Protein: 28g

BEEF WITH ZUCCHINI NOODLES

INGREDIENTS

- 1 teaspoon fresh ginger, grated
- 2 medium garlic cloves, minced
- 1/4 cup coconut aminos
- 2 tablespoons fresh lime juice
- 1 ½ pound NY strip steak, trimmed and sliced thinly
- 2 medium zucchini, spiralized with blade C
- Salt to taste
- 2 tablespoons essential olive oil
- 2 medium scallions, sliced
- 1 teaspoon red pepper flakes, crushed
- 2 tablespoons fresh cilantro, chopped

DIRECTIONS

1. In a big bowl, mix ginger, garlic, coconut aminos and lime juice. Add the beef and coat with the marinade generously. Refrigerate to marinade for approximately 10 minutes.
2. Set zucchini noodles over a large paper towel and sprinkle with salt.
3. Keep aside for around 10 minutes.
4. In a big skillet, heat oil on a medium-high heat. Add the scallions and red pepper flakes then saute for about 1 minute.
5. Add the beef with the marinade and stir fry for around 3-4 minutes or till browned.
6. Stir in the fresh cilantro, then add the zucchini and cook for approximately 3-4 minutes.
7. Serve hot.

15 minutes

9 minutes

4

NUTRITION

Calories per serving: 437; Carbohydrates: 9g; Fats: 22 g; Protein: 32g

10 minutes

22 minutes

5

SPICED GROUND BEEF

INGREDIENTS

- 2 tablespoons coconut oil
- 2 whole garlic cloves
- 2 whole cardamoms
- 1 (2 inches) piece cinnamon stick
- 2 bay leaves
- 1 teaspoon cumin seeds
- 2 onions, chopped
- Salt to taste
- 1/2 tablespoon garlic paste
- 1/2 tablespoon fresh ginger paste
- 1 pound lean ground beef
- 1 ½ teaspoon powdered fennel seeds
- 1 teaspoon ground cumin
- 1 ½ teaspoon red chili powder
- 1/8 teaspoon ground turmeric
- Freshly ground black pepper, to taste
- 1 cup coconut milk
- 1/4 cup water
- 1/4 cup fresh cilantro, chopped

DIRECTIONS

1. In a sizable pan, heat oil on a medium heat. Mix cloves, cardamoms, cinnamon stick, bay leaves and cumin seeds; cook for about 20 seconds.
2. Add the onion and 2 pinches of salt then saute for about 3-4 minutes.
3. Add the garlic-ginger paste and stir fry for about 2 minutes.
4. Add the beef and cook for about 4-5 minutes, entering pieces using the spoon. Stir in spices and cook.
5. Set in the coconut milk and water; cook for about 7-8 minutes. Flavor with salt and take away from the heat.
6. Serve hot using the garnish of cilantro.

NUTRITION

Calories per serving: 219; Protein: 20g; Fats: 11g; Carbohydrates: 5.4g

15 minutes

60 minutes

6

BEEF GOULASH

INGREDIENTS

- 1 lb. chuck steak, trim the fat and cut into bite-sized pieces
- 1 orange pepper, chopped
- 1 red pepper, chopped
- 1 green pepper, chopped
- 3 onions, quartered
- 3 garlic cloves, finely chopped
- 1 cup low-sodium beef broth
- 1 can tomatoes, chopped
- 2 tablespoons tomato paste
- 3 cups water
- 2 bay leaves
- 1 tablespoon paprika
- 1 tablespoon olive oil
- 2 teaspoons hot smoked paprika
- sea salt and black pepper to taste

DIRECTIONS

1. Heat your oil in a soup pot over a medium-high heat. Add the steak and cook until browned, stirring often.
2. Add your onions, and continue to cook for another 5 minutes or until soft. Add the garlic and cook for another minute, stirring often.
3. Add your remaining ingredients, then bring to a boil. Reduce the heat to a low simmer for 50 minutes, stirring occasionally. The Goulash is done when the steak is tender. Stir well, then add to serving bowls and enjoy!

NUTRITION

Calories per serving: 290; Fats: 9g; Protein: 31g; Carbohydrates: 13g

CAJUN BEEF & RICE SKILLET

INGREDIENTS

- 2 cups cauliflower rice, cooked
- ¾ lb. lean ground beef
- 1 red bell pepper, thinly sliced
- 1 jalapeno pepper, with seeds removed and finely diced
- 1 celery stalk, thinly sliced
- ½ yellow onion, diced
- ¼ cup fresh parsley, finely chopped
- 4 teaspoons Cajun seasoning
- ½ cup low-sodium beef broth

DIRECTIONS

1. Place the beef along with 1 ½ teaspoon of Cajun seasoning into a large skillet over medium-high heat.
2. Add the vegetables, except cauliflower and remaining Cajun seasoning. Cook, occasionally stirring, for about 8 minutes or until the vegetables are tender.
3. Add the broth and stir, and cook for 3 minutes or until the mixture has thickened. Stir in your cauliflower rice and cook until heated through. Remove from the heat and add to serving bowls, then top with parsley, serve and enjoy!

10 minutes

25 minutes

4

NUTRITION

Calories per serving: 69; Fats: 3g ; Protein: 7g ; Carbohydrates: 3g

10 minutes

8 minutes

2

BEEF TENDERLOIN & AVOCADO CREAM

INGREDIENTS

- 1 teaspoon mustard
- 2 (6 ounces) beef steaks
- ¼ cup sour cream
- 2 teaspoons lemon juice, fresh
- 1/3 avocado
- 1 tablespoon olive oil
- sea salt along with fresh ground black pepper as needed

DIRECTIONS

1. Preheat your oven to 450° Fahrenheit.
2. Sprinkle the beef steaks with some salt and pepper.
3. Mix the mustard and oil and spread the mixture over the meat.
4. Place the steaks in a skillet over medium-high heat for 3 minutes.
5. Transfer the steaks to a baking sheet and place in the oven, then bake for 6 minutes.
6. Blend the avocado with lemon juice and sour cream.
7. Serve steaks with avocado cream and enjoy!

NUTRITION

Calories per serving: 102 ; Protein: 13.5g ; Fats: 17.5g; Carbohydrates: 27g

BEEF AND RED BEAN CHILI

INGREDIENTS

- 1 cup of dried red beans
- 1 tablespoon olive oil
- 1 pounds boneless beef chuck
- 1 large onion, coarsely chopped
- 1 (14 ounce) can beef broth
- 2 chipotle chili peppers in adobo sauce
- 2 teaspoons dried oregano, crushed
- 1 teaspoon ground cumin
- ½ teaspoon salt
- 1 (14.5 ounce) can tomatoes with mild green chilis
- 1 (15 ounce) can tomato sauce
- ¼ cup snipped fresh cilantro
- 1 medium sweet red pepper

DIRECTION

1. Rinse out the beans and place them in a Dutch oven or big saucepan, then add enough water to cover them. Allow the beans to boil then reduce the heat. Simmer the beans without a lid for 10 minutes. Remove from the heat and keep covered for an hour.
2. In a large frying pan, heat the oil on a medium-high heat, then cook onions and half the beef until they brown a bit over medium-high heat. Move into a 3 1/2- or 4-quart slow cooker. Do this again with what's left of the beef. Add in tomato sauce, tomatoes (not drained), salt, cumin, oregano, adobo sauce, chipotle peppers, and broth, stirring to blend. Strain out and rinse beans and stir in the cooker.
3. Cook while covered on a low setting for around 10-12 hours or on high setting for 5-6 hours. Spoon the chili into bowls or mugs and top with sweet pepper and cilantro.

10 minutes

6 hours

4

NUTRITION

Calories per serving: 404; Fats: 22g; Carbohydrate: 4g; Protein: 27g

GROUND BEEF WITH VEGGIES

60 minutes

22 minutes

4

INGREDIENTS

- 1-2 tablespoons coconut oil
- 1 red onion,
- 2 red jalapeño peppers
- 2 minced garlic cloves
- 1 pound lean ground beef
- 1 small head broccoli, chopped
- 1/2 head cauliflower
- 3 carrots, peeled and sliced
- 3 celery ribs
- Chopped fresh thyme, to taste
- Dried sage, to taste
- Ground turmeric, to taste
- Salt and freshly ground black pepper

DIRECTIONS

1. In a large skillet, dissolve the coconut oil on medium heat.
2. Stir in the onion, jalapeño peppers and garlic. Saute for about 5 minutes.
3. Add the beef and cook for around 4-5 minutes, stirring from time to time.
4. Add the remaining ingredients and cook, stirring occasionally for about 8-10 minutes.
5. Serve hot.

NUTRITION

Calories per serving: 136 ; Carbohydrates: 9g ; Fats: 5g ; Protein: 17

GROUND BEEF WITH GREENS AND TOMATOES

15 minutes

15 minutes

4

INGREDIENTS

- 1 tablespoon organic olive oil
- 1/2 white onion, chopped
- 2 garlic cloves, finely chopped
- 1 jalapeño pepper, finely chopped
- 1 pound lean ground beef
- 1 teaspoon ground coriander
- 1 teaspoon ground cumin
- 1/2 teaspoon ground turmeric
- 1/2 teaspoon ground ginger
- 1/2 teaspoon ground cinnamon
- 1/2 teaspoon ground fennel seeds
- Salt and freshly ground black pepper
- 8 fresh cherry tomatoes, quartered
- 8 collard green leaves, stemmed and chopped
- 1 teaspoon fresh lemon juice

DIRECTIONS

1. In a big skillet, heat oil on medium heat.
2. Add the onion and saute for approximately 4 minutes.
3. Stir in the garlic and jalapeño pepper. Saute for approximately 1 minute.
4. Add the beef and spices; cook for approximately 6 minutes breaking into pieces while using a spoon.
5. Set in tomatoes and greens. Cook, stirring gently for about 4 minutes.
6. Whisk in lemon juice and remove from the heat.

NUTRITION

Calories per serving: 260; Fats: 16g ; Carbohydrates: 5 g ; Protein: 25 g

ZUCCHINI BEEF SAUTÉ WITH CORIANDER GREENS

INGREDIENTS

- 10 ounces beef, sliced into 1-2 inch strips
- 1 zucchini, cut into 2-inch strips
- ¼ cup parsley, chopped
- 3 garlic cloves, minced
- 2 tablespoons tamari sauce
- 4 tablespoons avocado oil

DIRECTIONS

1. Add 2 tablespoons avocado oil in a frying pan over high heat.
2. Place strips of beef and brown for a few minutes on high heat.
3. Once the meat is brown, add zucchini strips and sauté until tender.
4. Once tender, add tamari sauce, garlic, parsley and let them sit for a few minutes more.
5. Serve immediately and enjoy!

10 minutes

10 minutes

4

NUTRITION

Calories per serving: 218 ; Fats: 17g ; Carbohydrates: 1g; Protein: 12.5g

CHARRED SIRLOIN WITH CREAMY HORSERADISH SAUCE

INGREDIENTS

- 1-3 tablespoons of horseradish (from a jar)
- 6 tablespoons of low-fat sour cream
- Seasoning or salt, pepper, garlic, and onion to taste
- 1 pound sirloin steaks, trimmed with the visible fat removed

DIRECTIONS

1. Preheat the grill to a medium-high temperature.
2. On all sides, season the steak.
3. Turn on the grill and cook on either side for about 5-7 minutes, based on how thin the steak is and how fried you like your beef. For rare, you'll leave it on for less time and for medium-well, more. Using a meat thermometer is the perfect way to prepare your steak.
4. When the meat is cooked, mix the sour cream and horseradish to make the sauce. To create a sauce consistency, add water, one teaspoon at a time. Put aside until needed.
5. When the steak is cooked to your liking, leave it to rest for 5 minutes, then slice thinly.

5 minutes

15 minutes

4

NUTRITION

Calories per serving: 225; Protein: 24g ; Fats: 12.2g ; Carbohydrates: 2g

Chapter 3
Legume Recipes

5 minutes

50 minutes

10

KALE WHITE BEAN SOUP

INGREDIENTS

- 2 tablespoons olive oil
- 1 sweet onion, chopped
- 2 celery stalk, sliced
- 2 carrots, diced
- 1 fennel bulb, sliced
- 2 garlic cloves, chopped
- 2 cans cannellini beans, drained
- 1 thyme sprig
- ¼ teaspoon chili flakes
- ½ teaspoon dried marjoram
- 4 cups vegetable stock
- 4 cups water
- 8 kale leaves, shredded
- Salt and pepper to taste

DIRECTIONS

1. Heat the oil in a soup pot and stir in the onion, celery, carrots, fennel and garlic.
2. Cook for 5 minutes then stir in the beans, chili flakes, marjoram, stock, water, salt and pepper.
3. Cook for 20 minutes then add the kale. Cook for another 5 minutes then serve the soup hot.

NUTRITION

Calories per serving: 46 ; Fats: 1.6g ; Protein: 1.9g ; Carbohydrates: 5.7g

GARLIC AND PARSLEY CHICKPEAS

INGREDIENTS

- ¼ cup extra-virgin olive oil, divided
- 4 garlic cloves, sliced thinly
- 1/8 teaspoon red pepper flakes
- 1 onion, finely choppedly
- ¼ teaspoon of salt, plus more to taste
- Black pepper, to taste
- 2 (15-ounce / 425-g) cans chickpeas, rinsed
- 1 cup vegetable broth
- 2 tablespoons chopped fresh parsley
- 2 teaspoons lemon juice

DIRECTIONS

1. Add 3 tablespoons of the olive oil, garlic, and pepper flakes to a skillet over medium heat.
2. Cook for about 3 minutes, stirring constantly, or until the garlic turns golden but not brown.
3. Stir in the onion and ¼ teaspoon of salt and cook for 5 to 7 minutes, or until softened and lightly browned.
4. Add the chickpeas and broth to the skillet and bring to a simmer.
5. Reduce the heat to medium-low, cover, and cook for about 7 minutes, or until the chickpeas are cooked through.
6. Uncover, increase the heat to high and continue to cook for about 3 minutes more, or until nearly all the liquid has evaporated.
7. Turn off the heat and stir in the parsley and lemon juice. Season to taste with salt and pepper and drizzle with the remaining 1 tablespoon of olive oil.
8. Serve hot.

10 minutes

18-20 mins

4 to 6

NUTRITION

Calories per serving: 254 ; Fats: 11g ; Protein: 8g ; Carbohydrates: 27g

GREEK CHICKPEAS WITH CORIANDER AND SAGE

30 minutes

10' + Brining Time

6 to 8

INGREDIENTS

- 1½ tablespoons table salt, for brining
- 1 pound (2½ cups) dried chickpeas, picked over and rinsed
- 2 tablespoons extra-virgin olive oil, plus extra for drizzling
- 2 onions, halved and thinly sliced
- ¼ teaspoon of table salt
- 1 tablespoon of coriander seeds, cracked
- ¼–½ teaspoon red pepper flakes
- 2½ cups chicken broth
- ¼ cup fresh sage leaves
- 2 bay leaves
- 1½ teaspoons grated lemon zest plus 2 teaspoons of juice
- 2 tablespoons fresh chopped parsley

DIRECTIONS

1. Dissolve 1½ tablespoons of salt in 2 quarts of cold water in a large container. Add chickpeas and marinade at room temperature for at least 8 hours or up to 24 hours. Drain and rinse well.
2. Using the highest sauté function, heat oil in a pressure cooker until shimmering. Add onions and ¼ teaspoon of salt and cook until onions are softened and well browned, about 10 to 12 minutes.
3. Stir in coriander and pepper flakes and cook until fragrant (about 30 seconds). Stir in broth, scraping up any browned bits, then stir in chickpeas, sage, and bay leaves.
4. Lock the lid in place and close the pressure release valve. Select the low pressure cook function and cook for 10 minutes.
5. Turn off the pressure cooker and let the pressure release naturally for 15 minutes. Quick-release any remaining pressure, then carefully remove the lid, allowing steam to escape away from you.
6. Discard bay leaves. Stir lemon zest and juice into chickpeas and season with salt and pepper to taste. Sprinkle with parsley. Serve, drizzling individual portions with extra oil.

NUTRITION

Calories per serving: 300 ; Total Fats: 7g; Carbohydrates: 42g ; Protein: 15g

BARLEY WITH LENTILS, MUSHROOMS, AND TAHINI-YOGURT SAUCE

INGREDIENTS

- ½ ounce dried porcini mushrooms, rinsed
- 1 cup pearl barley
- ½ cup black lentils, picked over and rinsed
- 2 tablespoons extra-virgin olive oil
- 1 onion, finely chopped
- 2 large portobello mushroom caps, cut into 1-inch pieces
- 3 (2-inch) strips of lemon zest, sliced thin lengthwise
- ¾ teaspoon ground coriander
- Salt and pepper
- 2 tablespoons chopped fresh dill
- ½ cup Tahini-Yogurt Sauce

DIRECTIONS

Preparing the Ingredients

1. Microwave 1½ cups of water and porcini mushrooms in a covered bowl until steaming, (about 1 minute).
2. Let the mushrooms sit until softened (about 5 minutes).
3. Drain mushrooms in a fine-mesh strainer lined with a coffee filter, reserving marinating liquid, and chop the mushrooms.
4. Bring 4 quarts of water to boil in a Dutch oven. Add barley, lentils, and 1 tablespoon of salt, return to the boil and cook until tender (20 to 40 minutes).
5. Drain barley and lentils, return to the now-empty pot, and cover to keep warm.
6. Meanwhile, heat oil in a 12-inch nonstick skillet over medium heat until shimmering. Add onion and cook until softened (about 5 minutes).
7. Stir in portobello mushrooms, cover, and cook until the portobellos have released their liquid and have begun to brown (about 4 minutes).
8. Uncover, stir in lemon zest, coriander, ½ teaspoon salt, and ¼ teaspoon pepper, and cook until fragrant, about 30 seconds.
9. Stir in porcini and the porcini marinating liquid, bring to the boil, and cook, stirring occasionally, until the liquid is thickened slightly and reduced to ½ cup (about 5 minutes).
10. Stir the mushroom mixture and dill into the barley-lentil mixture and season with salt and pepper to taste. Serve, drizzling individual portions with Tahini-Yogurt Sauce.

5 minutes

45 minutes

4

NUTRITION

Calories per serving: 162 ; Fats: 0.75g ; Carbohydrates: 31g; Protein: 11g

42

5 minutes

50 minutes

4 to 6

FRENCH LENTILS WITH CARROTS AND PARSLEY

INGREDIENTS

- 2 carrots, peeled and finely chopped
- 1 onion, finely chopped
- 1 celery rib, finely chopped
- 2 tablespoons extra-virgin olive oil
- Salt and pepper
- 2 garlic cloves, minced
- 1 teaspoon minced fresh thyme or ¼ teaspoon dried
- 2½ cups water
- 1 cup lentilles du Puy, picked over and rinsed
- 2 tablespoons fresh parsley, finely chopped
- 2 teaspoons lemon juice

DIRECTIONS

1. Combine carrots, onion, celery, 1 tablespoon oil, and ½ teaspoon salt in a large saucepan. Cover and cook over a medium-low heat, stirring occasionally, until vegetables are softened, (8 to 10 minutes). Stir in garlic and thyme and cook until fragrant (about 30 seconds).
2. Stir in water and lentils and bring to a simmer. Reduce heat to low, cover, and simmer gently, stirring occasionally, until lentils are mostly tender (40 to 50 minutes).
3. Uncover and continue to cook, stirring occasionally, until lentils are completely tender, about 8 minutes. Stir in remaining 1 tablespoon oil, parsley, and lemon juice. Season with salt and pepper to taste and serve.

NUTRITION

Calories per serving: 118; Fats: 6g ; Carbohydrates: 13g ; Protein: 4g

CHICKPEAS WITH GARLIC AND PARSLEY

INGREDIENTS

- 1/4 cup extra-virgin olive oil
- 4 garlic cloves, sliced thin
- 1/8 teaspoon red pepper flakes
- 1 onion, finely chopped
- Salt and pepper
- 2 (15-ounce) cans chickpeas, rinsed
- 1 cup chicken or vegetable broth
- 2 tablespoons minced fresh parsley
- 2 teaspoons lemon juice

DIRECTIONS

1. Cook 3 tablespoons of oil, garlic, and pepper flakes in a 12-inch skillet over medium heat, stirring frequently, until the garlic turns golden but not brown, about 3 minutes. Stir in the onion and ¼ teaspoon salt and cook until softened and lightly browned, 5 to 7 minutes. Stir in chickpeas and broth and bring to a simmer.
2. Reduce the heat to medium-low, cover, and cook until chickpeas are heated through and flavors combine, about 7 minutes.
3. Uncover, increase heat to high, and continue to cook until nearly all liquid has evaporated, about 3 minutes. Off the heat, stir in parsley and lemon juice.
4. Season with salt and pepper to taste and drizzle with the remaining 1 tablespoon of oil. Serve.

5 minutes

10 minutes

4 to 6

NUTRITION

Calories per serving: 392 ; Fats: 15g ; Carbohydrates: 50g ; Protein: 16g

44

5 minutes

35 minutes

4 to 6

SPICY CHICKPEAS WITH TURNIPS

INGREDIENTS

- 2 tablespoons extra-virgin olive oil
- 2 onions, chopped
- 2 red bell peppers, stemmed, seeded, and chopped
- Salt and pepper
- ¼ cup tomato paste
- 1 jalapeño chili, stemmed, seeded, and finely chopped
- 5 garlic cloves, minced
- ¾ teaspoon ground cumin
- ¼ teaspoon cayenne pepper
- 2 (15-ounce) cans chickpeas
- 12 ounces turnips, peeled and cut into ½-inch pieces
- ¾ cup water, plus extra as needed
- ¼ cup chopped fresh parsley
- 2 tablespoons lemon juice, plus extra for seasoning

DIRECTIONS

1. Heat oil in a Dutch oven over a medium heat until shimmering. Add onions, bell peppers, ½ teaspoon salt, and ¼ teaspoon pepper and cook until softened and lightly browned, 5 to 7 minutes. Stir in tomato paste, jalapeño, garlic, cumin, and cayenne and cook until fragrant, about 30 seconds.
2. Stir in chickpeas and their liquid, turnips, and water. Bring to a simmer and cook until turnips are tender and the sauce has thickened, 25 to 35 minutes.
3. Stir in parsley and lemon juice. Season with salt, pepper, and extra lemon juice to taste. Adjust consistency with extra hot water as needed.

NUTRITION

Calories per serving: 392 ; Fats: 11g ; Carbohydrates: 60g ; Protein: 18g

45

5 minutes

None

6

CHICKPEA SALAD WITH CARROTS, ARUGULA, AND OLIVES

INGREDIENTS

- 2 (15-ounce) cans chickpeas, rinsed
- 1/4 cup extra-virgin olive oil
- 2 tablespoons lemon juice
- Salt and pepper
- Pinch cayenne pepper
- 3 carrots, peeled and shredded
- 1 cup baby arugula, coarsely chopped
- 1/2 cup pitted kalamata olives, coarsely chopped

DIRECTIONS

1. Microwave chickpeas in a medium bowl until hot, for about 2 minutes. Stir in oil, lemon juice, ¾ teaspoon salt, ½ teaspoon pepper, and cayenne and let this sit for 30 minutes.
2. Add carrots, arugula, and olives and toss to combine. Season with salt and pepper to taste. Serve.

NUTRITION

Calories per serving: 150; Fats: 11.5g ; Carbohydrates: 45g ; Protein: 1.4g

CHICKPEA AND HUMMUS PATTIES IN PITAS

INGREDIENTS

- 1 can chickpeas, drained and rinsed
- 1/2 cup lemony garlic hummus or ½ cup prepared hummus
- 1/2 cup whole-wheat panko breadcrumbs
- 1 large egg
- 2 teaspoons dried oregano
- 1/4 teaspoon freshly ground black pepper
- 1 tablespoon extra-virgin olive oil
- 1 cucumber, unpeeled (or peeled if desired), cut in half lengthwise
- 1 (6-ounce / 170-g) container of 2% plain Greek yogurt
- 1 garlic clove, minced
- 2 whole-wheat pita breads, cut in half
- 1 medium tomato, cut into 4 thick slices

DIRECTIONS

1. In a large bowl, mash the chickpeas with a potato masher or fork until coarsely smashed (they should still be somewhat chunky).
2. Add the hummus, breadcrumbs, egg, oregano, and pepper. Stir well to combine.
3. With your hands, form the mixture into 4 (½-cup-size) patties. Press each patty flat to about ¾ inch thick and put on a plate.
4. In a large skillet over medium-high heat, heat the oil until very hot, for about 3 minutes. Cook the patties for 5 minutes, then flip with a spatula. Cook for an additional 5 minutes.
5. While the patties are cooking, shred half of the cucumber with a box grater or finely chop with a knife.
6. In a small bowl, stir together the shredded cucumber, yogurt, and garlic to make the tzatziki sauce.
7. Slice the remaining half of the cucumber into ¼-inch-thick slices and set aside.
8. Toast the pita breads.
9. To assemble the sandwiches, lay the pita halves on a work surface. Into each pita, place a few slices of cucumber, a chickpea patty, and a tomato slice, then drizzle the sandwich with the tzatziki sauce and serve.

15 minutes

13 minutes

4

NUTRITION

Calories per serving: 520 ; Fats: 12g ; Protein: 26g ; Carbohydrates: 84g

LENTIL SALAD WITH OLIVES, MINT, AND FETA

5 minutes

60 minutes

4 to 6

INGREDIENTS

- Salt and pepper
- 1 cup of Puy lentils, picked over and rinsed
- 5 garlic cloves, lightly crushed and peeled
- 1 bay leaf
- 5 tablespoons extra-virgin olive oil
- 3 tablespoons white wine vinegar
- ½ cup pitted kalamata olives, coarsely chopped
- ½ cup chopped fresh mint
- 1 large shallot, minced
- 1-ounce feta cheese, crumbled (¼ cup)

DIRECTIONS

Preparing the Ingredients

1. Dissolve 1 teaspoon salt in 4 cups of hot water (about 110 degrees) in a bowl. Add lentils and marinade at room temperature for 1 hour. Drain well. Move the oven rack to the middle position and heat the oven to 325 degrees. Combine lentils, 4 cups water, garlic, bay leaf, and ½ teaspoon salt in a medium ovenproof saucepan.
2. Cover, transfer the saucepan to the oven, and cook until the lentils are tender but remain intact, 40 to 60 minutes.
3. Drain lentils well, discarding the garlic and bay leaf.
4. In a large bowl, whisk oil and vinegar together. Add lentils, olives, mint, and shallot and toss to combine. Season with salt and pepper to taste. Transfer to a serving dish and sprinkle with feta. Serve hot or at room temperature.

NUTRITION

Calories per serving: 215; Fats: 17g ; Carbohydrates: 12g; Protein: 5g

SPICY CHICKPEAS WITH TURNIPS

INGREDIENTS

- 2 tablespoons extra-virgin olive oil
- 2 onions, chopped
- 2 red bell peppers, stemmed, seeded, and chopped
- Salt and pepper
- ¼ cup tomato paste
- 1 jalapeño chile, stemmed, seeded, and finely chopped
- 5 garlic cloves, minced
- ¾ teaspoon ground cumin
- ¼ teaspoon cayenne pepper
- 2 (15-ounce) cans chickpeas
- 12 ounces turnips, peeled and cut into ½-inch pieces
- ¾ cup water, plus extra as needed
- ¼ cup chopped fresh parsley
- 2 tablespoons lemon juice, plus extra for seasoning

DIRECTIONS

1. Heat oil in a Dutch oven over medium heat until shimmering. Add onions, bell peppers, ½ teaspoon salt, and ¼ teaspoon pepper and cook until softened and lightly browned, 5 to 7 minutes. Stir in tomato paste, jalapeño, garlic, cumin, and cayenne and cook until fragrant, about 30 seconds.
2. Stir in chickpeas and their liquid, turnips, and water. Bring to a simmer and cook until turnips are tender and sauce has thickened, 25 to 35 minutes.
3. Stir in parsley and lemon juice. Season with salt, pepper, and extra lemon juice to taste. Adjust the consistency with extra hot water as needed.

5 minutes

35 minutes

4 to 6

NUTRITION

Calories per serving: 381 ; Fats: 10g ; Carbohydrates: 60g; Protein: 17g

CHICKPEA SALAD WITH CARROTS, ARUGULA, AND OLIVES

INGREDIENTS

- 2 (15-ounce) cans chickpeas, rinsed
- 1/4 cup extra-virgin olive oil
- 2 tablespoons lemon juice
- Salt and pepper
- Pinch cayenne pepper
- 3 carrots, peeled and shredded
- 1 cup baby arugula, coarsely chopped
- 1/2 cup pitted kalamata olives, coarsely chopped

DIRECTIONS

1. Microwave chickpeas in a medium bowl until hot, for about 2 minutes. Stir in oil, lemon juice, ¾ teaspoon salt, ½ teaspoon pepper, and cayenne and let sit for 30 minutes.
2. Add carrots, arugula, and olives and toss to combine. Season with salt and pepper to taste. Serve.

5 minutes

None

6

NUTRITION

Calories per serving: 303; Fats: 9g ; Carbohydrates: 45g ; Protein: 12g

COCONUT CURRY LENTILS

10 minutes

40 minutes

4

INGREDIENTS

- 1 cup brown lentils
- 1 small white onion, peeled and chopped
- 1 teaspoon minced garlic
- 1 teaspoon grated ginger
- 3 cups baby spinach
- 1 tablespoon of curry powder
- 2 tablespoons olive oil
- 13 ounces coconut milk, unsweetened
- 2 cups vegetable broth

For Serving:

- 4 cups cooked rice
- ¼ cup chopped cilantro

DIRECTIONS

1. Put oil in your large pot over medium heat, and when hot, add ginger and garlic and cook for 1 minute until fragrant.
2. Add onion, cook for 5 minutes, stir in curry powder, cook for 1 minute until toasted, add lentils and pour in the broth.
3. Switch the heat to a medium-high level, bring the mixture to a boil, then turn down the heat to a lower level and simmer for 20 minutes until tender and all the liquid is absorbed.
4. Pour in milk, stir until combined, turn down the heat to a medium level, and simmer for 10 minutes until thickened.
5. Remove the pot, stir in the spinach, let it stand for 5 minutes until its leaves have wilted and then top with cilantro. Serve lentils with rice.

NUTRITION

Calories per serving: 236 ; Fats: 9g; Carbohydrates: 35g; Protein: 6g

---

TOMATO, KALE, AND WHITE BEAN SKILLET

10 minutes

10 minutes

4

INGREDIENTS

- 30 ounces cooked cannellini beans
- 3 1/2 ounces sun-dried tomatoes, chopped, packed in oil
- 6 ounces kale, chopped
- 1 teaspoon minced garlic
- 1/4 teaspoon ground black pepper
- 1/4 teaspoon salt
- 1/2 tablespoon dried basil
- 1/8 teaspoon red pepper flakes
- 1 tablespoon apple cider vinegar
- 1 tablespoon olive oil
- 2 tablespoons oil from sun-dried tomatoes

DIRECTIONS

1. Prepare the dressing and for this, place basil, black pepper, salt, vinegar, and red pepper flakes in a small bowl, add oil from the sun-dried tomatoes and whisk until combined.
2. Take a skillet pan, place it over medium heat, add olive oil and when hot, add garlic and cook for 1 minute until fragrant.
3. Add kale, splash with some water and cook for 3 minutes until kale leaves have wilted. Add tomatoes and beans, stir well and cook for 3 minutes until heated.
4. Remove the pan from the heat, drizzle with the prepared dressing, toss until mixed and serve.

NUTRITION

Calories per serving: 242 ; Fats: 7.5g; Carbohydrates: 42g; Protein: 5g

CHARD WRAPS WITH MILLET

52

INGREDIENTS

- 1 carrot, cut into ribbons
- 1/2 cup millet, cooked
- 1/2 of a large cucumber, cut into ribbons
- 1/2 cup chickpeas, cooked
- 1 cup of sliced cabbage
- 1/3 cup of hummus
- Mint leaves as needed for topping
- Hemp seeds as needed for topping
- 1 bunch of Swiss rainbow chard

DIRECTIONS

1. Spread hummus on one side of the chard.
2. Place some of the millet, vegetables, and chickpeas on top.
3. Sprinkle with some mint leaves and hemp seeds and wrap it like a burrito.
4. Serve straight away.

25 minutes

0 minute

4

NUTRITION

Calories per serving: 127; Fats: 4.7g; Carbohydrates: 16g; Protein: 4g

---

BROWN RICE TABBOULEH

53

INGREDIENTS

- 3 cups brown rice, cooked
- ¾ cup cucumber, chopped
- ¾ cup tomato, chopped
- ¼ cup mint leaves, chopped
- ¼ cup green onions, sliced
- ¼ cup olive oil
- ¼ cup lemon juice
- Salt, pepper, to taste

DIRECTIONS

1. Combine all ingredients in a large bowl. Toss well and chill for 20 mins.

20 minutes

0 minutes

6

NUTRITION

Calories per serving: 162; Carbohydrates: 18g; Fat: 9g; Protein: 2g

54

5 minutes

18 minutes

6

CHICKPEA NOODLE SOUP

INGREDIENTS

- 1 cup cooked chickpeas
- 8 ounces rotini noodles, whole-wheat
- 4 celery stalks, sliced
- 2 medium white onions, peeled, chopped
- 4 medium carrots, peeled, sliced
- 2 teaspoons minced garlic
- 8 sprigs of thyme
- 1 teaspoon salt
- 1/3 teaspoon ground black pepper
- 1 bay leaf
- 2 tablespoons olive oil
- 2 cups of vegetable broth
- ¼ cup chopped fresh parsley

DIRECTIONS

1. Heat a large pot over medium heat.
2. Add oil and, when hot, add all the vegetables.
3. Stir in garlic, thyme and a bay leaf and cook for 5 minutes until vegetables are golden and sautéd.
4. Then pour in the broth, stir and bring the mixture to boil.
5. Add the chickpeas and noodles to the boiling soup and continue cooking for 8 minutes until the noodles are tender. Then season the soup with salt and black pepper.
6. Garnish with parsley and serve straight away

NUTRITION

Calories per serving: 153 ; Fats: 6g ; Carbohydrates: 20g ; Protein: 3g

CHORIZO-KIDNEY BEANS QUINOA PILAF

INGREDIENTS

- ¼ pound of dried Spanish chorizo diced (about 2/3 cup)
- ¼ teaspoon red pepper flakes
- ¼ teaspoon smoked paprika
- ½ teaspoon cumin
- ½ teaspoon sea salt
- 1 3/4 cups water
- 1 cup quinoa
- 1 large clove garlic, minced
- 1 small red bell pepper finely diced
- 1 small red onion finely diced
- 1 tablespoon tomato paste
- 15-ounce can kidney beans rinsed and drained

DIRECTIONS

1. Place a nonstick pot on medium high heat and heat for 2 minutes. Add chorizo and sauté for 5 minutes until lightly browned.
2. Stir in peppers and the onion. Sauté for 5 minutes.
3. Add tomato paste, red pepper flakes, salt, paprika, cumin, and garlic. Sauté for 2 minutes.
4. Stir in quinoa and mix well. Sauté for 2 minutes.
5. Add water and beans. Mix well. Cover and simmer for 20 minutes or until the liquid is fully absorbed.
6. Turn off the heat and fluff the quinoa. Let it sit for 5 minutes more, uncovered.
7. Serve and enjoy.

10 minutes

35 minutes

4

NUTRITION

Calories per serving: 213 ; Protein: 12g ; Carbohydrates: 23g; Fats: 8g

QUICK SHRIMP FETTUCCINE

10 minutes

10 minutes

4

INGREDIENTS

- 8 oz. fettuccine pasta
- 1/4 cup extra-virgin olive oil
- 3 tbsp. garlic, minced
- 1 lb. large shrimp (21-25), peeled and deveined
- 1/3 cup lemon juice
- 1 tbsp. lemon zest
- 1/2 tsp. salt
- 1/2 tsp. freshly ground black pepper

DIRECTIONS

1. Bring a large pot of salted water to a boil. Add the fettuccine and cook for 8 minutes.
2. In a large saucepan over medium heat, cook the olive oil and garlic for 1 minute.
3. Add the shrimp to the saucepan and cook for 3 minutes on each side. Remove the shrimp from the pan and set aside.
4. Add the lemon juice and lemon zest to the saucepan, along with the salt and pepper.
5. Reserve ½ cup of the pasta water and drain the pasta.
6. Add the pasta water to the saucepan with the lemon juice and zest and stir everything together. Add the pasta and toss together to evenly coat the pasta. Transfer the pasta to a serving dish and top with the cooked shrimp. Serve hot.

NUTRITION

Calories per serving: 216 ; Protein: 8g ; Carbohydrates: 32g ; Fats: 4g

---

GARLIC SHRIMP FETTUCCINE

10 minutes

15 minutes

4 to 6

INGREDIENTS

- 8 ounces fettuccine pasta
- 1/4 cup extra-virgin olive oil
- 3 tablespoons garlic, minced
- 1 pound large shrimp, peeled and deveined
- 1/3 cup lemon juice
- 1 tablespoon lemon zest
- 1/2 teaspoon salt
- 1/2 teaspoon freshly ground black pepper

DIRECTIONS

1. Bring a large pot of salted water to a boil. Add the fettuccine and cook for 8 minutes. Reserve ½ cup of the cooking liquid and drain the pasta.
2. In a large saucepan over medium heat, heat the olive oil. Add the garlic and sauté for 1 minute.
3. Add the shrimp to the saucepan and cook each side for 3 minutes. Remove the shrimp from the pan and set aside.
4. Add the remaining ingredients to the saucepan. Stir in the cooking liquid. Add the pasta and toss together to evenly coat the pasta.
5. Transfer the pasta to a serving dish and serve topped with the cooked shrimp.

NUTRITION

Calories per serving: 240 ; Fats: 11g ; Protein: 24g ; Carbohydrates: 9g

ROASTED RATATOUILLE PASTA

INGREDIENTS

- 1 small eggplant (about 8 ounces / 227 g)
- 1 small zucchini
- 1 portobello mushroom
- 1 Roma tomato, halved
- ½ medium sweet red pepper, seeded
- ½ teaspoon salt, plus additional for the pasta water
- 1 teaspoon Italian herb seasoning
- 1 tablespoon olive oil
- 2 cups farfalle pasta (about 8 ounces / 227 g)
- 2 tablespoons minced sun-dried tomatoes in olive oil with herbs
- 2 tablespoons prepared pesto

DIRECTIONS

1. Slice the ends off the eggplant and zucchini. Cut them lengthwise into ½-inch slices.
2. Place the eggplant, zucchini, mushroom, tomato, and red pepper in a large bowl and sprinkle with ½ teaspoon of salt. Using your hands, toss the vegetables well so that they're covered evenly with the salt. Let them rest for about 10 minutes.
3. While the vegetables are resting, preheat the oven to 400°F (205°C). Line a baking sheet with parchment paper.
4. When the oven is hot, drain off any liquid from the vegetables and pat them dry with a paper towel. Add the Italian herb seasoning and olive oil to the vegetables and toss well to coat both sides.
5. Lay the vegetables out in a single layer on the baking sheet. Roast them for 15 to 20 minutes, flipping them over after about 10 minutes or once they start to brown on the underside. When the vegetables are charred in spots, remove them from the oven.
6. While the vegetables are roasting, fill a large saucepan with water. Add salt and cook the pasta until al dente, about 8 to 10 minutes. Drain the pasta, reserving ½ cup of the pasta water.
7. When cool enough to handle, cut the vegetables into large chunks (about 2 inches) and add them to the hot pasta.
8. Stir in the sun-dried tomatoes and pesto and toss everything well. Serve immediately.

10 minutes

30 minutes

2

NUTRITION

Calories per serving: 520; Fats: 30g ; Protein: 11.5g; Carbohydrates: 57g

LENTIL AND MUSHROOM PASTA

10 minutes

50 minutes

2

INGREDIENTS

- 2 tablespoons olive oil
- 1 large yellow onion, finely diced
- 2 portobello mushrooms, trimmed and finely choppedly
- 2 tablespoons tomato paste
- 3 garlic cloves, chopped
- 1 teaspoon oregano
- 2½ cups water
- 1 cup brown lentils
- 1 (28-ounce / 794-g) can diced tomatoes with basil (with juice if diced)
- 1 tablespoon balsamic vinegar
- 8 ounces (227 g) pasta of choice, cooked
- Salt and black pepper, to taste
- Chopped basil, for garnish

DIRECTIONS

1. Place a large stockpot over medium heat. Add the oil. Once the oil is hot, add the onion and mushrooms. Cover and cook until both are soft, about 5 minutes. Add the tomato paste, garlic, and oregano and cook 2 minutes, stirring constantly.
2. Stir in the water and lentils. Bring to a boil, then reduce the heat to medium-low and cook for 5 minutes, covered.
3. Add the tomatoes (and juice if using diced) and vinegar. Replace the lid, reduce the heat to low and cook until the lentils are tender, about 30 minutes.
4. Remove the sauce from the heat and season with salt and pepper to taste. Garnish with the basil and serve over the cooked pasta.

NUTRITION

Calories per serving: 495; Fats: 24g ; Protein: 63g; Carbohydrates: 35g

AUTHENTIC PASTA E FAGIOLI

INGREDIENTS

- 2 tablespoons olive oil
- 1 teaspoon garlic, pressed
- 4 small-sized potatoes, peeled and diced
- 1 parsnip, chopped
- 1 carrot, chopped
- 1 celery rib, chopped
- 1 leek, chopped
- 1 (6-ounce) can tomato paste
- 4 cups water
- 2 vegetable bouillon cubes
- 8 ounces cannellini beans, marinated overnight
- 6 ounces elbow pasta
- 1/2 teaspoon oregano
- 1/2 teaspoon basil
- 1/2 teaspoon fennel seeds
- Sea salt, to taste
- 1/4 teaspoon freshly cracked black pepper
- 2 tablespoons Italian parsley, roughly chopped

DIRECTIONS

1. Press the "Sauté" button to preheat a pressure cooker. Heat the oil and sauté the garlic, potatoes, parsnip, carrot, celery, and leek until they have softened.
2. Now, add in the tomato paste, water, bouillon cubes, cannellini beans, elbow pasta, oregano, basil, fennel seeds, freshly cracked black pepper, and sea salt.
3. Secure the lid. Choose the "Manual" mode and cook for 9 minutes at High pressure. Once cooking is complete, use a quick pressure release; carefully remove the lid.
4. Serve with fresh Italian parsley. Bon appétit!

6 minutes

15 minutes

4

NUTRITION

Calories per serving: 455; Fats: 8g; Carbohydrates: 82g; Protein: 15g

ESCAROLE AND CANNELLINI BEANS ON PASTA

20 minutes

25 minutes

8

INGREDIENTS

- Pepper and salt to taste
- 1 can 14.5-oz diced tomatoes with garlic and onion, drained
- 1 can 15.5-oz cannellini beans, with liquid
- 1 head escarole chopped
- 1 package 16-oz dry penne pasta

DIRECTIONS

1. Cook pasta according to package instructions, then drain and rinse under cold running water.
2. On medium high heat, place skillet and cook diced tomatoes, cannellini beans with liquid and escarole.
3. Season with pepper and salt and cook until boiling.
4. Remove from the heat and mix pasta.
5. Serve and enjoy.

NUTRITION

Calories per serving: 126; Carbohydrates: 21g; Protein: 9g; Fats: 0.2g

BEEF WITH TOMATO SPAGHETTI

10 minutes

20 minutes

4

INGREDIENTS

- 12 ounces spaghetti
- Zest and juice from 1 lemon
- 2 garlic cloves, minced
- 2 tablespoons olive oil
- 1-pound beef, ground
- Salt and black pepper to taste
- 1-pint cherry tomatoes, chopped
- 1 small red onion, chopped
- ½ cup white wine
- 2 tablespoons tomato paste
- Some basil leaves, chopped for serving
- Some parmesan, grated for serving

DIRECTIONS

1. Put water in a large saucepan, add a pinch of salt, bring to the boil over a medium-high heat, add spaghetti, cook according to instructions, drain and return the pasta to the pan.
2. Add lemon zest and juice and 1 tablespoon of oil to the pasta, toss to coat, heat up over medium heat for a couple of seconds, divide between plates and keep warm.
3. Meanwhile, heat a pan with the remaining oil over a medium heat, add garlic, stir and cook for 1 minute.
4. Add beef, salt, and pepper and brown it for 4 minutes.
5. Add tomato paste and wine, stir and cook for 3 minutes.
6. Divide beef on plates, add tomatoes, red onion, basil, and parmesan and serve.

NUTRITION

Calories per serving: 360 ; Protein: 28g ; Fats: 16g ; Carbohydrates: 26g

SPAGHETTI WITH ANCHOVY SAUCE

INGREDIENTS

- Salt
- 0.75 lb spaghetti
- 1/4 cup extra-virgin olive oil
- 1 can oil-packed anchovy fillets, undrained
- 3 garlic cloves, minced
- 1/4 cup chopped fresh flat-leaf parsley
- 1 teaspoon red pepper flakes
- 1/4 teaspoon freshly ground black pepper
- 1 tablespoon breadcrumbs

DIRECTIONS

1. Bring a large pot of water to a boil over high heat. Once boiling, salt the water to your liking, stir, and return to a boil. Add the spaghetti and cook according to package directions until al dente. Drain, reserving about ½ cup of the cooking water.
2. Meanwhile, in a large skillet, heat the olive oil over low heat. Add the anchovy fillets with their oil and the garlic. Cook for 7 to 10 minutes, until the pasta, is ready, stirring until the anchovies melt away and form a sauce.
3. Add the spaghetti, parsley, red pepper flakes, black pepper, and a little of the reserved cooking water, as needed, and toss to combine all the ingredients.
4. Sprinkle with the breadcrumbs.

5 minutes

10 minutes

4

NUTRITION

Calories per serving: 207 ; Fats: 3g ; Protein: 8g ; Carbohydrates: 30g

Chapter 5
Poultry Recipes

64

5 minutes

15 minutes

4

HEARTY LEMON AND PEPPER CHICKEN

INGREDIENTS

- 2 teaspoons olive oil
- 0.75 pounds skinless chicken cutlets
- 2 whole eggs
- ¼ cup panko breadcrumbs
- 1 tablespoon lemon pepper
- Sunflower seeds and pepper to taste
- 3 cups green beans
- ¼ cup parmesan cheese
- ¼ teaspoon garlic powder

DIRECTIONS

1. Pre-heat your oven to 425 degrees F.
2. Take a bowl and stir in seasoning, parmesan, lemon pepper, garlic powder and panko breadcrumbs.
3. Whisk eggs in another bowl.
4. Coat cutlets in eggs and press into the panko breadcrumb mix.
5. Transfer coated chicken to a parchment lined baking sheet.
6. Toss the beans in oil, pepper, add sunflower seeds, and lay them on the side of the baking sheet.
7. Bake for 15 minutes.
8. Enjoy!

NUTRITION

Calorie: 262; Fats:11g; Carbohydrates: 9g; Protein: 32g

65

30 minutes

1h 20'

6

LEMON GARLIC CHICKEN

INGREDIENTS

- 6 chicken breast fillets
- 3 tablespoons olive oil
- 1 tablespoon lemon juice
- 3 cloves garlic, crushed and minced
- 2 teaspoon dried parsley

DIRECTIONS

1. Marinate the chicken breast fillets in a mixture of olive oil, lemon juice, garlic, parsley, and a pinch of salt and pepper.
2. Let sit for 1 hour covered in the refrigerator.
3. Press the sauté setting in the pressure cooker.
4. Pour in the vegetable oil.
5. Cook the chicken for 5 minutes per side or until fully cooked.

NUTRITION

Calories per serving: 394 ; Fats: 13g ; Carbohydrate: 0.15g ; Protein: 64g

TURKEY WITH BASIL & TOMATOES

INGREDIENTS

- 4 turkey breast fillets
- 1 tablespoon olive oil
- 1/4 cup fresh basil, chopped
- 1/2 cups cherry tomatoes, sliced in half
- 1/4 cup olive tapenade

NUTRITION CALORIES 238

Fats: 13g; Carbohydrate: 3g; Protein: 30g

DIRECTIONS

1. Season the turkey fillets with salt.
2. Add the olive oil to the pressure cooker.
3. Set it to sauté.
4. Cook the turkey until brown on both sides.
5. Stir in the basil, tomatoes and olive tapenade.
6. Cook for 3 minutes, stirring frequently.

10 minutes

20 minutes

4

TURKEY AND CRANBERRY SAUCE

INGREDIENTS

- 1 cup chicken stock
- 2 tablespoons avocado oil
- ½ cup cranberry sauce
- 1 big turkey breast, skinless, boneless, and sliced
- 1 yellow onion, roughly chopped
- Salt and black pepper to taste

NUTRITION

Calories per serving: 205 ; Fats: 14g ; Carbohydrates: 5g; Protein: 6g

DIRECTIONS

1. Heat the oven to 350 degrees F.
2. Place the avocado oil in a pan and heat over a medium-high heat.
3. Add the onion and sauté for 5 minutes.
4. Add the turkey and brown for 5 minutes more.
5. Add the rest of the ingredients and toss.
6. Place in the oven and cook for 40 minutes

10 minutes

50 minutes

4

68

10 minutes

40 minutes

4

SAGE TURKEY MIX

INGREDIENTS

- 1 big turkey breast, skinless, boneless, and roughly cubed
- Juice of 1 lemon
- 2 tablespoons avocado oil
- 1 red onion, chopped
- 2 tablespoons sage, chopped
- 1 garlic clove, minced
- 1 cup chicken stock

DIRECTIONS

1. Heat up a pan with the avocado oil over a mmedium-high heat, add the turkey, and brown for 3 minutes on each side.
2. Add the rest of the ingredients, bring to a simmer and cook over medium heat for 35 minutes.
3. Divide the mixture between plates and serve with a side dish.

NUTRITION

Calories 231; Fat 9.5g; Carbohydrates: 4g; Protein 9g

69

15 minutes

55 minutes

4

ROASTED CHICKEN THIGHS

INGREDIENTS

- 8 chicken thigths
- 3 tbsp. fresh parsley, chopped
- 1 tsp. dried oregano
- 6 garlic cloves, crushed
- 10 oz. roasted red peppers, sliced
- 2 cups grape tomatoes
- ½ lbs. potatoes, cut into small chunks
- 4 tbsp. olive oil
- Pepper
- Salt

DIRECTIONS

1. Heat the oven at 400 F.
2. Season the chicken thighs with pepper and salt.
3. Heat 2 tablespoons of olive oil in a pan over medium heat. Add chicken to the pan and sear until lightly golden brown from all the sides.
4. Transfer the chicken onto a baking tray. Add tomato, potatoes, oregano, garlic, and red peppers around the chicken. Season with pepper and salt and drizzle with remaining olive oil.
5. Bake in the preheated oven for 45-55 minutes.
6. Garnish with parsley and serve.

NUTRITION

Calories per serving: 508; Fats: 20g; Protein: 52g; Carbohydrates: 58g

CHICKEN WITH POTATOES, OLIVES & SPROUTS

INGREDIENTS

- 1 lb. chicken breasts, skinless, boneless, and cut into pieces
- ¼ cup olives, quartered
- 1 tsp. oregano
- 1 ½ tsp. Dijon mustard
- 1 lemon juice
- 1/3 cup vinaigrette dressing
- 1 medium onion, diced
- 3 cups potatoes cut into pieces
- 4 cups Brussels sprouts, trimmed and quartered
- ¼ tsp. pepper
- ¼ tsp. salt

DIRECTIONS

1. Heat the oven to 400 F.
2. Place the chicken in the center of the baking tray, then place potatoes, sprouts, and onions around the chicken.
3. In a small bowl, mix vinaigrette, oregano, mustard, lemon juice, and salt and pour over chicken and veggies. Sprinkle olives and season with pepper.
4. Bake in a preheated oven for 20 minutes.
5. Transfer the chicken to a plate. Stir the vegetables and roast for 15 minutes more. Serve and enjoy.

15 minutes

35 minutes

4

NUTRITION

Calories per serving: 341; Fats: 6.5g; Protein: 37g; Carbohydrates: 41g

CHICKEN SHAHEATA

INGREDIENTS

- 2 lb. chicken breast, sliced into strips
- 1 teaspoon of paprika
- 1 teaspoon of ground cumin
- 1/4 teaspoon of garlic granules
- 1/2 teaspoon of turmeric
- 1/4 teaspoon of ground allspice

DIRECTIONS

1. Season the chicken with the spices, and a little salt and pepper.
2. Pour 1 cup of chicken broth to the pot.
3. Seal the pot.
4. Choose the poultry setting.
5. Cook for 15 minutes.
6. Release the pressure naturally.

15 minutes

30 minutes

8

NUTRITION

Calories per serving: 146; Fats 3.3g; Carbohydrate 2.6g; Protein 26g

AMAZING GRILLED CHICKEN AND BLUEBERRY SALAD

10 minutes

25 minutes

5

INGREDIENTS

- 5 cups mixed greens
- 1 cup blueberries
- ¼ cup sliced almonds
- 2 cups chicken breasts, cooked and cubed

For dressing

- ¼ cup olive oil
- ¼ cup apple cider vinegar
- ¼ cup blueberries
- 2 tablespoons honey
- Sunflower seeds and pepper to taste

DIRECTIONS

1. Take a bowl and add greens, berries, almonds, chicken cubes and mix well.
2. Take a bowl and mix the dressing ingredients, pour the mix into a blender and blitz until smooth.
3. Add dressing on top of the chicken cubes and toss well.
4. Season more and enjoy!

NUTRITION

Calories per serving: 126 ; Fats: 4.6g ; Carbohydrates: 9g ; Protein: 14g

---

GARLIC MUSHROOM CHICKEN

15 minutes

15 minutes

4

INGREDIENTS

- 4 chicken breasts, boneless and skinless
- 3 garlic cloves, minced
- 1 onion, chopped
- 2 cups mushrooms, sliced
- 1 tbsp olive oil
- ½ cup chicken stock
- ¼ tsp pepper
- ½ tsp salt

DIRECTIONS

1. Season the chicken with pepper and salt. Heat the oil in a pan on medium heat, then put the seasoned chicken in the pan and cook for 5-6 minutes on each side. Remove and place on a plate.
2. Add onion and mushrooms to the pan and sauté until tender, about 2-3 minutes. Add garlic and sauté for a minute. Add stock and bring to a boil. Stir well and cook for 1-2 minutes. Pour over chicken and serve.

NUTRITION

Calories per serving: 233; Fats: 6g; Protein: 21g; Carbohydrates: 4g

WHITE CHICKEN CHILI

INGREDIENTS

- 1 can white chunk chicken
- 2 cans low-sodium white beans, drained
- 1 can low-sodium diced tomatoes
- 4 cups of low-sodium chicken broth
- 1 medium onion, chopped
- 1/2 medium green pepper, chopped
- 1 medium red pepper, chopped
- 2 garlic cloves, minced
- 2 teaspoons chili powder
- 1 teaspoon ground cumin
- 1 teaspoon dried oregano
- Cayenne pepper, to taste
- 8 tablespoons shredded reduced-fat Monterey Jack cheese
- 3 tablespoons chopped fresh cilantro

DIRECTIONS

1. In a soup pot, add beans, tomatoes, chicken, and chicken broth.
2. Cover and let it simmer over medium heat. Meanwhile, grease a nonstick pan with cooking spray. Add peppers, garlic, and onions. Sauté for 5 minutes until soft.
3. Transfer the mixture to the soup pot. Add cumin, chili powder, cayenne pepper, and oregano.
4. Cook for 10 minutes, then garnish the chili with cilantro and 1 tablespoon cheese. Serve.

20 minutes

15 minutes

4

NUTRITION

Calories per serving: 133 ; Fats: 3g ; Carbohydrates: 11g ; Protein: 12.5g

SWEET POTATO-TURKEY MEATLOAF

15 minutes

25 minutes

4

INGREDIENTS

- 1 large sweet potato, peeled and cubed
- 1-pound ground turkey (breast)
- 1 large egg
- 1 small sweet onion, finely chopped
- 2 cloves garlic, minced
- 2 slices whole-wheat breadcrumbs
- ¼ cup honey barbecue sauce
- ¼ cup ketchup
- 2 tablespoons Dijon Mustard
- 1 tablespoon fresh ground pepper
- ½ tablespoon salt

DIRECTIONS

1. Heat the oven to 350 F. Grease a baking dish. In a large pot, boil a cup of lightly salted water and add the sweet potato. Cook until tender. Drain the water. Mash the potato.
2. Mix the honey barbecue sauce, ketchup, and Dijon mustard in a small bowl. Mix thoroughly. In a large bowl, mix the turkey and the egg. Add the sweet onion and garlic. Pour in the sauce mixture. Add the breadcrumbs. Season the mixture with salt and pepper.
3. Add the sweet potato. Combine thoroughly with your hands. If the mixture feels wet, add more breadcrumbs. Shape the mixture into a loaf. Place in the loaf pan. Bake for 25 – 35 minutes until the meat is cooked through. Broil for 5 minutes. Slice and serve.

NUTRITION

Calories per serving: 281; Protein: 26.5g ; Carbohydrates: 18g ; Fats: 9.5g

HOT CHICKEN WINGS

15 minutes

25 minutes

4

INGREDIENTS

- 10 - 20 chicken wings
- ½ stick of margarine
- 1 bottle of Durkee hot sauce
- 2 tablespoons of honey
- 10 shakes of Tabasco sauce
- 2 tablespoons of cayenne pepper

DIRECTIONS

1. Heat canola oil in a deep pot. Deep-fry the wings until cooked, approximately 20 minutes. Mix the hot sauce, honey, Tabasco, and cayenne pepper in a medium bowl. Mix well.
2. Place the cooked wings on paper towels. Drain the excess oil. Mix the chicken wings in the sauce until coated evenly.

NUTRITION

Calories per serving: 475; Protein: 29g ; Carbohydrates: 16g ; Fats: 34g

CRISPY CASHEW CHICKEN

INGREDIENTS

- 2 chicken breasts, skinless, boneless
- 2 egg whites
- 1 cup of cashew nuts
- ¼ cup of breadcrumbs
- 2 cups of peanut oil or vegetable oil
- ¼ cup of corn starch
- 1 teaspoon of brown sugar
- 2 teaspoons of salt
- 1 teaspoon of dry sherry

DIRECTIONS

1. Heat the oven to 400 F. Put the cashews in a blender. Pulse until they are finely chopped. Place in a shallow bowl and stir in the breadcrumbs.
2. Wash the chicken breasts. Pat them dry. Cut into small cubes. In a separate shallow bowl, mix the salt, corn starch, brown sugar, and sherry. In a separate bowl, beat the egg white.
3. Put the oil into a large, deep pot. Heat to a high temperature. Place the chicken pieces on a plate. Arrange the bowls in a row; flour, eggs, cashews & breadcrumbs. Prepare a baking tray with parchment paper.
4. Dunk the chicken pieces in the flour, then the egg, and then the cashew mixture. Shake off the excess mixture. Gently place the chicken in the oil. Fry on each side for 2 minutes. Place on the baking tray.
5. Once done, slide the baking tray into the oven. Cook for 4 minutes, flip and then cook for an additional 4 minutes, until golden brown. Serve immediately, or cold, with your favorite low-fat dip.

15 minutes

30 minutes

5

NUTRITION

Calories per serving: 130; Protein: 15g ; Carbohydrates: 11g ; Fats: 4.6g

CHICKEN TORTELLINI SOUP

15 minutes

30 minutes

5

INGREDIENTS

- 2 chicken breasts, boneless, skinless; diced into cubes
- 1 tablespoon of flavorless oil (olive oil, canola, sunflower)
- 1 teaspoon of butter
- 2 cups of cheese tortellini
- 2 cups of frozen broccoli
- 2 cans of cream of chicken soup
- 4 cups of water
- 1 large onion, diced
- 2 garlic cloves, minced
- 2 large carrots, sliced
- 1 celery stick, sliced
- 1 teaspoon of oregano
- ½ teaspoon of basil

DIRECTIONS

1. Pull the broccoli out of the freezer. Set in a bowl.
2. Rinse and pat dry the chicken breasts. Then dice them into cubes.
3. In a large pot, heat the oil. Fry the cubes of chicken breast. Remove them from the pot and place on them on kitchen paper to drain off the oil.
4. Add the teaspoon of butter to the hot pot. Sauté the onion, garlic, carrots, and celery, broccoli. Once the vegetables are el dente, add the chicken soup and water. Stir the ingredients until they are combined. Bring to a simmer.
5. Add the chicken and tortellini back to the pot. Cook on low for 10 minutes, or until the tortellini is cooked. Serve immediately.

NUTRITION

Calories per serving: 255; Protein: 31g ; Carbohydrates: 19g ; Fats: 5.4g

CHICKEN DIVAN

15 minutes

30 minutes

4

INGREDIENTS

- 1/2-pound cooked chicken, boneless, skinless, diced in bite-size pieces
- 1 cup broccoli, cooked, diced into bite-size pieces
- 1 cup extra sharp cheddar cheese, grated
- 1 can of mushroom soup
- ½ cup of water
- 1 cup of croutons

DIRECTIONS

1. Heat the oven to 350 F. In a large pot, heat the soup and water.
2. Add the chicken, broccoli, and cheese. Combine thoroughly.
3. Pour into a greased baking dish. Place the croutons over the mixture.
4. Bake for 30 minutes or until the casserole is bubbling, and the croutons are golden brown.

NUTRITION

Calories per serving: 180; Protein: 20g ; Carbohydrates: 11g ; Fats: 6.7g

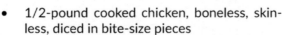

CREAMY CHICKEN FRIED RICE

INGREDIENTS

- 2 pounds of chicken; white and dark meat (diced into cubes)
- 2 tablespoons of butter or margarine
- 1 ½ cups of instant rice
- 1 cup of mixed frozen vegetables
- 1 can of condensed cream of chicken soup
- 1 cup of water
- 1 cube of instant chicken bouillon
- Salt and pepper to taste

DIRECTIONS

1. Take the vegetables out of the freezer. Set aside.
2. Heat a large, deep skillet over medium heat and add the butter or margarine.
3. Place the chicken in the skillet and season with salt and pepper. Fry until both sides are brown.
4. Remove the chicken, then adjust the heat and add the rice. Add the water and bouillon.
5. Cook the rice, then add the chicken and the vegetables. Mix in the soup, then simmer until the vegetables are tender. Serve immediately.

15 minutes

45 minutes

4

NUTRITION

Calories per serving: 285; Protein: 46g ; Carbohydrates: 16g ; Fats: 6g

CHICKEN TIKKA

INGREDIENTS

- 4 chicken breasts, skinless, boneless; cubed
- 2 large onion, cut into chunks
- 10 cherry tomatoes
- 1/3 cup plain non-fat yogurt
- 4 garlic cloves, crushed
- 1 ½ inch of fresh ginger, peeled and chopped
- 1 small onion, grated
- 1 ½ teaspoon chili powder
- 1 tablespoon of ground coriander
- 1 teaspoon of salt
- 2 tablespoons of coriander leaves

DIRECTIONS

1. In a large bowl, combine the non-fat yogurt, grated onion, crushed garlic, ginger, chili powder, coriander, salt, and pepper. Add the cubed chicken and stir until the chicken is coated.
2. Cover with plastic film and place in the fridge. Marinate for 2 – 4 hours.
3. Heat the broiler or barbecue.
4. After marinating the chicken, get some skewers ready. Alternate pieces of chicken, cherry tomatoes and onion chunks onto the skewers.
5. Grill for 6 – 8 minutes on each side. Once the chicken is cooked through, pull the meat and vegetables off the skewers and put onto plates. Garnish with coriander. Serve immediately.

15 minutes

20 minutes

6

NUTRITION

Calories per serving: 160 ; Protein: 11.5g ; Carbohydrates: 8.3g ; Fats: 3.5g

HONEY SPICED CAJUN CHICKEN

15 minutes

20 minutes

4

INGREDIENTS

- 2 chicken breasts, skinless and boneless
- 1 tablespoon of butter or margarine
- 1 pound of linguini
- 3 large mushrooms, sliced
- 1 large tomato, diced
- 2 tablespoons of regular mustard
- 4 tablespoons of honey
- 3 ounces of low-fat table cream
- Parsley, roughly chopped

DIRECTIONS

1. Wash and dry the chicken breasts.
2. Heat 1 tablespoon of butter or margarine in a large pan. Add the chicken breasts. Season with salt and pepper. Cook on each side for 6 – 10 minutes, until cooked thoroughly.
3. Remove the chicken breasts from the pan. Set aside.
4. Cook the linguine - as stated on the packet - in a large pot.
5. Save 1 cup of the pasta water and then drain the linguine.
6. Add the mushrooms and tomatoes to the pan that the chicken was cooked in. Heat until they are tender.
7. Add the honey, mustard, and cream. Combine thoroughly. Add the chicken and linguine to the pan. Stir until coated. Garnish with parsley. Serve immediately.

NUTRITION

Calories per serving: 490; Protein: 44.5g ; Carbohydrates: 57.5g ; Fats: 7g

HEALTHY CHICKEN

15 minutes

35 minutes

4

INGREDIENTS

- 4 chicken breasts, skinless and boneless
- 1 large jar of low sodium pasta sauce
- 1 tablespoon of flavorless oil (olive, canola, or sunflower)
- 1 large onion, diced
- 1 large green pepper, diced
- ½ teaspoon garlic salt
- Salt and pepper to taste
- 1 cup low-fat mozzarella cheese, grated
- A handful of spinach leaves, washed, dried and roughly chopped

DIRECTIONS

1. Wash the chicken breasts and pat dry.
2. In a large pot, heat the oil. Add the onion and cook until it sweats and becomes translucent.
3. Add the chicken. Season with salt, pepper, and garlic salt.
4. Cook the chicken for 6 – 10 minutes on each side.
5. Add the peppers. Cook for 2 minutes. Pour the pasta sauce over the chicken. Mix well. Simmer on low for 20 minutes.
6. Serve on plates, sprinkle the cheese over each piece. Garnish with spinach.

NUTRITION

Calories per serving: 218 ; Protein: 30g ; Carbohydrates: 17g ; Fats: 4.7g

LEMON-PARSLEY CHICKEN BREAST

INGREDIENTS

- 2 chicken breasts, skinless and boneless
- 1/3 cup of white wine
- 1/3 cup of lemon juice
- 2 garlic cloves, minced
- 3 tablespoons of breadcrumbs
- 2 tablespoons of flavorless oil (olive, canola, or sunflower)
- ¼ cup fresh parsley

DIRECTIONS

1. Mix the wine, lemon juice and garlic in a measuring cup.
2. Pound each chicken breast until they are ¼ inch thick.
3. Coat the chicken with breadcrumbs, and heat the oil in a large skillet.
4. Fry the chicken breasts for 6 minutes on each side, until they turn brown.
5. Pour the wine mixture over the chicken. Simmer for 5 minutes.
6. Pour any extra juices over the chicken. Garnish with parsley.

15 minutes

15 minutes

2

NUTRITION

Calories per serving: 376; Protein: 64g ; Carbohydrates: 4g ; Fats: 6g

GARLIC PEPPER CHICKEN

INGREDIENTS

- 2 chicken breasts, cut into strips
- 2 bell peppers, cut into strips
- 5 garlic cloves, chopped
- 3 tbsp. water
- 2 tbsp. olive oil
- 1 tbsp. paprika
- 2 tsp. black pepper
- 1/2 tsp. salt

DIRECTIONS

1. Heat olive oil in a large saucepan over medium heat. Add garlic and sauté for 2-3 minutes. Add peppers and cook for 3 minutes.
2. Add chicken and spices and stir to coat. Add water and stir well.
3. Bring to the boil and then cover and simmer for 10-15 minutes.
4. Serve and enjoy.

15 minutes

21 minutes

2

NUTRITION

Calories per serving: 378; Fats: 9.5g; Protein: 63g; Carbohydrates: 7g

MUSTARD CHICKEN TENDERS

15 minutes

20 minutes

4

INGREDIENTS

- 1 lb. chicken tenders
- 2 tbsp. fresh tarragon, chopped
- 1/2 cup whole grain mustard
- 1/2 tsp. paprika
- 1 garlic clove, minced
- 1/2 oz. fresh lemon juice
- 1/2 tsp. pepper
- 1/4 tsp. kosher salt

DIRECTIONS

1. Heat the oven to 425 F.
2. Add all ingredients except for the chicken to the large bowl and mix well.
3. Put the chicken in the bowl, then stir until well coated.
4. Place chicken on a baking dish and cover. Bake for 15-20 minutes.
5. Serve and enjoy.

NUTRITION

Calories per serving: 317; Fats: 17g; Protein: 24g; Carbohydrates: 17g

SPICY MUSTARD CHICKEN

32 minutes

36 minutes

4

INGREDIENTS

- 4 chicken breasts
- 2 garlic cloves, crushed
- 1/3 cup of chicken broth
- 3 tbsp of Dijon mustard
- ½ tsp of chili powder

DIRECTIONS

1. Pre-heatthe over at 375 F
2. In a small bowl, mix the mustard, chicken broth, garlic and chili.
3. Marinate the chicken for 30 minutes.
4. Bake for 35 minutes.

NUTRITION

Calories per serving: 340; Fats: 7g ; Protein: 65 ; Carbohydrates: 0

THE ALMOND BREADED CHICKEN GOODNESS

INGREDIENTS

- 2 large chicken breasts, boneless and skinless
- 1/3 cup of lemon juice
- 1 ½ cups seasoned almond meal
- 2 tablespoons coconut oil
- Lemon pepper, to taste
- Parsley for decoration

DIRECTIONS

1. Slice the chicken breasts in half.
2. Pound out each half until ¼ inch thick.
3. Take a pan and place it over medium heat, add oil and heat.
4. Dip each chicken breast slice in lemon juice and let it sit for 2 minutes.
5. Turnover and then let the other side sit for 2 minutes as well.
6. Transfer to almond meal and coat both sides.
7. Add the coated chicken to the oil and fry for 4 minutes per side, making sure to sprinkle lemon pepper liberally.
8. Transfer to a paper lined sheet and repeat until all the chicken pieces are fried.
9. Garnish with parsley and enjoy!

15 minutes

15 minutes

3

NUTRITION

Calories per serving: 437 ; Fats: 23g ; Carbohydrates: 8g ; Protein: 53g

CORIANDER AND COCONUT CHICKEN

INGREDIENTS

- 2 pounds of chicken thighs, skinless, boneless, and cubed
- 2 tbsp. of olive oil
- Salt and black pepper to taste
- 3 tbsp. of coconut flesh, shredded
- 1 ½ tsp. of orange extract
- 1 tbsp. of ginger, grated
- ¼ cup of orange juice
- 2 tbsp. of chopped coriander
- 1 cup chicken stock
- ¼ tsp. red pepper flakes

DIRECTIONS

1. Heat the oil in a pan over a medium-high heat
2. Add the chicken and brown for 4 minutes on each side.
3. Add salt, pepper and the rest of the ingredients
4. Bring to a simmer and cook over a medium heat for 20 minutes.
5. Divide the mixture between plates and serve hot.

10 minutes

30 minutes

4

NUTRITION

Calories 280; Fats: 5g; Carbohydrates: 11g; Protein: 41g

COCONUT CHICKEN

INGREDIENTS

- A 6 oz. chicken fillet
- ¼ cup of sparkling water
- One egg
- 3 tbsp. coconut flakes
- 1 tbsp. of coconut oil
- 1 tsp. of Greek Seasoning

DIRECTIONS

1. Cut the chicken fillet into small pieces (nuggets).
2. Then crack the egg in the bowl and whisk.
3. Mix up together the egg and sparkling water.
4. Add Greek seasoning and stir gently.
5. Dip the chicken nuggets in the egg mixture and then coat in the coconut flakes.
6. Melt the coconut oil in the skillet and heat until it is shimmering.
7. Then add the prepared chicken nuggets.
8. Roast them for 1 minute each or until they are light brown.
9. Dry the cooked chicken nuggets with the help of paper towels and transfer them to serving plates.

NUTRITION

Calories per serving: 210; Fats: 4g ; Carbohydrates: 0.25g; Protein: 17g

10 minutes

5 minutes

4

10 minutes

30 minutes

4

GINGER CHICKEN DRUMSTICKS

INGREDIENTS

- Four chicken drumsticks
- One apple, grated
- 1 tbsp of curry paste
- 4 tbsp of milk
- 1 tsp of coconut oil
- 1 tsp of chili flakes
- ½ tsp of minced ginger

DIRECTIONS

1. Preheat the oven to 360F.
2. Mix together the grated apple, curry paste, milk, chili flakes, and minced garlic.
3. Put the coconut oil in the skillet and melt.
4. Add the apple mixture and stir well.
5. Then add chicken drumsticks and mix well.
6. Roast the chicken for 2 minutes on each side.
7. Place the skillet with the chicken drumsticks in the oven and bake for 25 minutes.

NUTRITION

Calories per serving: 92 ; Fats: 3g ; Carbohydrates: 7g ; Protein: 9g

ITALIAN CHICKEN

INGREDIENTS

- 1 carrot, chopped
- 1/2 lb. mushrooms
- 8 chicken thighs
- 1 cup of tomato sauce
- 3 cloves garlic, crushed

DIRECTIONS

1. Season the chicken with salt and pepper.
2. Cover and marinate for 30 minutes.
3. Press the sauté setting on the pressure cooker.
4. Add 1 tablespoon of ghee.
5. Cook the carrots and mushrooms until soft.
6. Add the tomato sauce and garlic.
7. Add the chicken, tomatoes and olives.
8. Cook and mix well.
9. Seal the pot.
10. Set it to manual.
11. Cook at high pressure for 10 minutes.
12. Release the pressure naturally.

NUTRITION

Calories per serving: 182; Fats: 8g ; Carbohydrate: 5g; Protein: 22g

30 minutes

6

10 minutes

CHICKEN AND TZAZIKI PITAS

INGREDIENTS

13. 4 pita breads
14. 10 oz chicken fillet, grilled
15. 1 cup of chopped lettuce
16. 8 teaspoons of tzaziki
17. Directions:

18. Cut each pita bread in half to make 8 pita pockets.
19. Then fill every pita pocket with chopped lettuce and tzatziki sauce.
20. Chop the chicken fillet and add it to the pita pocket.
21. Serve

NUTRITION

Calories 135; Fats: 3g; Carbohydrates: 16g; Protein: 11g

10 minutes

0 minutes

8

CHICKEN, PASTA AND SNOW PEAS

15 minutes

20 minutes

2

INGREDIENTS

- 1-pound of chicken breasts
- 2 ½ cups of penne pasta
- 1 cup of snow peas, trimmed and halved
- 1 teaspoon of olive oil
- 1 standard jar of tomato and basil pasta sauce
- Fresh ground pepper

DIRECTIONS

1. In a medium frying pan, heat the olive oil. Flavor the chicken breasts with salt and pepper. Cook the chicken breasts until cooked through (approximately 5 – 7 minutes on each side).
2. Cook the pasta, as stated in the instructions of the packet. Cook the snow peas with the pasta. Scoop 1 cup of the pasta water before draining the pasta and peas and setting them aside.
3. Once the chicken is cooked, slice diagonally. Return the chicken to the frying pan and add the pasta sauce.
4. If the mixture seems dry, add some of the pasta water until it reaches the desired consistency.
5. Heat, then divide into bowls. Serve immediately.

NUTRITION

Calories per serving: 635; Protein: 80g ; Carbohydrates: 50g ; Fats: 10g

---

CHICKEN WITH NOODLES

15 minutes

30 minutes

6

INGREDIENTS

- 4 chicken breasts, skinless and boneless
- 1-pound of pasta (angel hair, linguine, or ramen noodles)
- ½ teaspoon of sesame oil
- 1 tablespoon of canola oil
- 2 tablespoons of chili paste
- 1 onion, diced
- 2 garlic cloves, coarsely chopped
- ½ cup of low-salt soy sauce
- ½ medium cabbage, sliced
- 2 carrots, coarsely chopped

DIRECTIONS

1. Cook your pasta in a large pot. Mix the canola oil, sesame oil, and chili paste and heat for 25 seconds in another large pot. Add the onion and cook for 2 minutes. Add the garlic and fry for 20 seconds. Add the chicken and cook on both sides for 5 - 7 minutes, until cooked through.
2. Remove the mix from the pan and set aside. Add the cabbage and carrots and cook until they are tender. Pour everything back into the pan.
3. Add the pasta, pour in the soy sauce and combine thoroughly. Heat for 5 minutes. Serve immediately.

NUTRITION

Calories per serving: 416; Protein: 50g ; Carbohydrates: 41g ; Fats: 4g

CHICKEN CHILI

INGREDIENTS

- 3 tablespoons of vegetable oil
- 2 cloves of garlic, minced
- 1 green bell pepper, chopped
- 1 onion, chopped
- 1 stalk of celery, sliced
- 0.25 pounds of mushrooms, chopped
- 1-pound chicken breast
- 1 tablespoon of chili powder
- 1 teaspoon of dried oregano
- 1 teaspoon of ground cumin
- 1/2 teaspoon of paprika
- 1/2 teaspoon of cocoa powder
- 1/4 teaspoon of salt
- 1 pinch of crushed red pepper flakes
- 1 pinch of ground black pepper
- 1 (14.5 oz) can of tomatoes with juice
- 1 (19 oz) can of kidney beans

DIRECTION

1. Pour 2 tablespoons of the oil into a big skillet and put on a moderate heat. Add mushrooms, celery, onion, bell pepper and garlic, sautéing for 5 minutes. Put to one side.
2. Put the remaining 1 tablespoon of oil into the skillet. At high heat, cook the chicken until browned and its exterior turns firm. Transfer the vegetable mixture back into the skillet.
3. Stir in ground black pepper, hot pepper flakes, salt, cocoa powder, paprika, oregano, cumin and chili powder. Continue stirring for several minutes to avoid burning. Pour in the beans and tomatoes and bring the entire mixture to boiling point. Next, adjust the setting to a low heat. Place a lid on the skillet and leave it simmering for 15 minutes. Then, uncover the skillet and leave it simmering for a further 15 minutes.

6 minutes

1 hour

4

NUTRITION

Calories per serving: 311 ; Carbohydrates: 22g ; Protein: 34g ; Fats: 10g

4 minutes

4 hours

5

CHICKEN AND PEPPERONI

INGREDIENTS

- 3½ to 4 pounds of meaty chicken pieces
- 2 teaspoon of salt
- 1/8 teaspoon of black pepper
- 2 ounces of sliced pepperoni
- ¼ cup of sliced pitted ripe olives
- ½ cup of reduced-sodium chicken broth
- 1 tablespoon of tomato paste
- 1 teaspoon of dried Italian seasoning
- ½ cup of shredded part-skim mozzarella cheese (2 ounces)

DIRECTIONS

1. Put chicken into a 3 1/2 to 5-qt. slow cooker. Sprinkle pepper and salt on the chicken.
2. Cut the pepperoni slices in half. Put olives and pepperoni into the slow cooker.
3. In a small bowl, blend Italian seasoning, tomato paste and chicken broth together. Transfer the mixture into the slow cooker.
4. Cook with a lid on for 3-3 1/2 hours on high.
5. Transfer the olives, pepperoni and chicken onto a serving platter with a slotted spoon. Discard the cooking liquid. Sprinkle cheese over the chicken. Use foil to loosely cover and allow to sit for 5 minutes to melt the cheese.

NUTRITIONS

Calories per serving: 406; Carbohydrates: 3g ; Protein: 64g; Fats: 14g

CHICKEN, BARLEY, AND LEEK STEW

INGREDIENTS

- 1-pound of chicken thighs
- 1 tablespoon of olive oil
- 1 (49 ounce) can of reduced-sodium chicken broth
- 1 cup of regular barley (not quick-cooking)
- 2 medium leeks, halved lengthwise and sliced
- 2 medium carrots, thinly sliced
- 1½ teaspoons dried basil or Italian seasoning, crushed
- ¼ teaspoon of cracked black pepper

DIRECTION

1. In the big skillet, cook the chicken in hot oil till it becomes brown on all sides.
2. In the 4-5-qt. slow cooker, whisk the pepper, dried basil, carrots, leeks, barley, chicken broth and chicken.
3. Keep covered and cook on the high heat setting for 2 – 2.5 hours or till the barley softens. Sprinkle with the parsley or fresh basil prior to serving.

10 minutes

3 hours

NUTRITION

Calories per serving: 692; Carbohydrates: 22g ; Fats: 27g; Protein: 71g

2

CREAMY CHICKEN NOODLE SOUP

99

INGREDIENTS

- 1 (32 fluid ounce) container of reduced-sodium chicken broth
- 3 cups of water
- 2½ cups of chopped cooked chicken
- 3 medium carrots, sliced
- 3 stalks of celery
- 1½ cups of sliced fresh mushrooms
- ¼ cup of chopped onion
- 1½ teaspoons of dried thyme, crushed
- ¾ teaspoon of garlic-pepper seasoning
- 3 ounces of reduced-fat cream cheese (Neufchâtel), cut up
- 2 cups of dried egg noodles

DIRECTIONS

1. Mix together the garlic-pepper seasoning, thyme, onion, mushrooms, celery, carrots, chicken, water and broth in a 5 to 6-quart slow cooker.
2. Cover and let it cook for 6-8 hours on a low-heat setting.
3. Increase to a high-heat setting if you are using the low-heat setting. Mix in the cream cheese until blended.
4. Add the uncooked noodles. Cover and let it cook for an additional 20-30 minutes or just until the noodles become tender.

7 minutes

8 hours

4

NUTRITION

Calories per serving: 442; Carbohydrates: 17g; Fats: 17g; Protein: 54g

Chapter 6
Vegetable, Salad & Side Dish Recipes

100

25 minutes

26 minutes

4

OKRA AND TOMATO CASSEROLE

INGREDIENTS

- 1 lb. okra, trimmed
- 1 tomatoes, cut into wedges
- 1 garlic cloves, chopped
- 1 cup fresh parsley leaves, finely cut
- 1 tbsp. extra virgin olive oil

DIRECTIONS

1. Pre-heat the oven to 350 degrees F.
2. In a deep ovenproof baking dish, combine okra, sliced tomatoes, olive oil and garlic.
3. Toss to combine and bake for 45 minutes. Drizzle with parsley and serve.

NUTRITION

Calories per serving: 80; Fats: 0.75g ; Protein: 3g; Carbohydrates: 16

FIVE-BEAN CHILI

INGREDIENTS

- 2 tablespoons extra-virgin olive oil
- 1 medium onion, diced
- 1 green bell pepper, diced
- 2 garlic cloves, minced
- 1 (28-ounce) can no-salt-added crushed tomatoes
- 1 tablespoon chili powder
- 1 teaspoon ground cumin
- 1 (15-ounce) can no-salt-added black beans, drained and rinsed
- 1 (15-ounce) can no-salt-added pinto beans, drained and rinsed
- 1 (15-ounce) can no-salt-added kidney beans, drained and rinsed
- 1 (15-ounce) can no-salt-added navy beans, drained and rinsed
- 1 (15-ounce) can no-salt-added chickpeas, drained and rinsed
- 10 scallions, chopped

DIRECTIONS

1. In a large pot, heat the oil over medium-high heat.
2. Add the onion and bell pepper and cook for 5 to 7 minutes, or until the onion is translucent.
3. Add the garlic and cook for 1 minute. Stir in the crushed tomatoes, chili powder, cumin, black beans, pinto beans, kidney beans, navy beans, and chickpeas. Reduce the heat to a simmer and cook, stirring frequently, for 20 minutes to thicken slightly and blend the flavors.
4. Divide between 6 storage containers. Store the scallions separately. Top the chili with the scallions after reheating to serve.

10 minutes

30 minutes

6

NUTRITION

Calories per serving: 110; Fats: 3.5g ; Carbohydrates: 35g; Protein: 14.5g

GARLIC LOVERS' HUMMUS

INGREDIENTS

- 3 tbsps. Freshly squeezed lemon juice
- All-purpose salt-free seasoning
- 3 tbsps. Sesame tahini
- 4 garlic cloves
- 15 oz. no-salt-added garbanzo beans
- 2 tbsps. Olive oil

DIRECTIONS

1. Drain garbanzo beans and rinse well.
2. Place all the ingredients in a food processor and pulse until smooth.
3. Serve immediately or cover and refrigerate until serving.

2 minutes

0 minutes

12

NUTRITION

Calories per serving: 30; Fats: 0.5g; Carbohydrates: 5.5g; Protein: 1.7g

SUPER BOWL WITH EGGPLANT AND CHICKEN

3 minutes

8 minutes

4

INGREDIENTS

- 1 tablespoon of olive oil
- 1 leek, chopped
- 2 chicken breasts, diced
- 1 pound of eggplant, peeled and sliced
- A teaspoon of garlic paste
- 1/2 teaspoon of turmeric powder
- 1 teaspoon of red pepper flakes
- 1 cup of broth, preferably homemade
- 1 cup of tomatoes, puréed
- Kosher salt and ground black pepper, to taste

DIRECTIONS

1. Press the "Sauté" button to heat up a pressure cooker. Then, heat the oil. Cook the leeks until softened.
2. Now, add the chicken breasts; cook for 3 to 4 minutes or until they are no longer pink. Then, add the remaining ingredients; stir to combine well.
3. Secure the lid. Choose 'Poultry' mode and 'high pressure'; cook for 5 minutes.
4. Once the cooking is complete, use a natural pressure release and carefully remove the lid.
5. Divide your dish between serving bowls and serve hot. Bon appétit!

NUTRITION

Calories per serving: 177; Fats: 5g; Carbohydrates: 12g; Protein: 6g

ROASTED SWEET CARROTS

2 minutes

8 minutes

4

INGREDIENTS

- 1-lb. sliced carrots
- ¼ tsp. white pepper
- 2 tbsps. lime juice
- 4 tbsps. honey
- ¼ tsp. salt

DIRECTIONS

1. Preheat the pan to a temperature of 350°F (180°C).
2. In a bowl add honey, salt, pepper and lime juice and then mix.
3. Now add the carrots and toss to combine.
4. Place the carrots in the fryer basket and cook for 8 minutes.
5. Serve!

NUTRITION

Calories per serving: 69; Protein: 1.2 g; Fats: 0.25g; Carbohydrates: 17g

TOMATO AND AVOCADO SALAD

INGREDIENTS

- 1-pound of cherry tomatoes
- 2 avocados
- 1 sweet onion, chopped
- 2 tablespoons of lemon juice
- 1½ tablespoons of olive oil
- A handful of basil, chopped

DIRECTIONS

1. Mix the tomatoes with the avocados and the rest of the ingredients in a serving bowl, toss and serve right away!

10 minutes

0 minutes

4

NUTRITION

Calories per serving: 168 ; Fats: 11g; Protein: 3.5g; Carbohydrates: 17g

CHICKPEA SALAD

106

INGREDIENTS

- Cooked chickpeas (15 oz.)
- 1 diced Roma tomato
- ½ a green medium bell pepper, diced
- 1 tbsp of fresh parsley
- 1 small white onion
- ½ of minced garlic
- 1 lemon, juiced.

DIRECTIONS

1. Chop the tomato, green pepper, and onion.
2. Mince the garlic. Combine each of these in a salad bowl and toss well.
3. Cover the salad and chill for at least 15 minutes in the fridge.
4. Serve when ready.

15 minutes

0 minutes

4

NUTRITION

Calories per serving: 152; Fats: 2g; Protein: 4g; Carbohydrates: 20g

CAULIFLOWER SPRINKLED WITH CURRY

10 minutes

5 hours

4

INGREDIENTS

- 1 cauliflower head, florets separated
- 2 carrots, sliced
- 1 red onion, chopped
- ¾ cup of coconut milk
- 2 garlic cloves, minced
- 2 tablespoons of curry powder
- A pinch of salt and black pepper
- 1 tablespoon of red pepper flakes
- 1 teaspoon of garam masala

DIRECTIONS

1. In your slow cooker, mix all of the ingredients.
2. Cover and cook on high for 5 hours
3. Divide into bowls and serve.

NUTRITION

Calories per serving: 68; Fats: 1.2g ; Protein: 3.5g ; Carbohydrates: 13g

PORK AND GREENS SALAD

10 minutes

15 minutes

4

INGREDIENTS

- 1-pound of pork chops
- 8 ounces of white mushrooms, sliced
- ½ cup of Italian dressing
- 6 cups of mixed salad greens
- 6 ounces of jarred artichoke hearts, drained
- Salt and black pepper to taste
- ½ cup of basil, chopped
- 1 tablespoon of olive oil

DIRECTIONS

1. Add the oil to a pan and heat over medium-high heat.
2. Add the pork, and brown for 5 minutes.
3. Add the mushrooms, stir, and sauté for 5 minutes more.
4. Add the dressing, artichokes, salad greens, salt, pepper, and basil.
5. Cook for 4-5 minutes, divide everything into bowls and serve.

NUTRITION

Calories per serving: 188 ; Fats: 4.75g ; Protein: 29g ; Carbohydrates: 10g

ROASTED BROCCOLI SALAD

INGREDIENTS

- 1 lb. broccoli
- 3 tablespoons of olive oil
- 2 cups of cherry tomatoes
- 1 ½ teaspoons of honey
- 3 cups of wholegrain bread, cubed
- 1 tablespoon of balsamic vinegar
- ½ teaspoon of black pepper
- ¼ teaspoon of sea salt, fine
- grated parmesan for serving

DIRECTIONS

1. Set the oven to 450 F, and then heat up a rimmed baking sheet.
2. Drizzle your broccoli with a tablespoon of oil, and toss to coat.
3. Take out the baking sheet from the oven, and spoon the broccoli onto it.
4. Put the rest of the oil into the bottom of a bowl and add your tomatoes.
5. Toss them to coat, then mix tomatoes with a tablespoon of honey. Place on the baking sheet with the broccoli.
6. Roast for fifteen minutes, and stir halfway through your cooking time.
7. Add your bread and then roast for three more minutes.
8. Whisk two tablespoons of oil, vinegar, and the remaining honey. Season. Pour this over your broccoli mix to serve.

9 minutes

17 minutes

4

NUTRITION

Calories per serving: 281 ; Protein: 8g ; Fats: 12g ; Carbohydrates: 38.5g

CHICKEN AND QUINOA SALAD

INGREDIENTS

- 2 tablespoons of olive oil
- 2 ounces of quinoa
- 2 ounces of cherry tomatoes, cut in quarters
- 3 ounces of sweet corn
- Lime juice from 1 lime
- Lime zest from 1 lime, grated
- 2 spring onions, chopped
- A small red chili pepper, chopped
- 1 avocado
- 2 ounces chicken meat

DIRECTIONS

1. Fill water in a pan and bring it to a boil over a medium-high heat
2. Add quinoa, stir and cook for 12 minutes.
3. Meanwhile, put the sweetcorn in a pan and heat over a medium-high heat.
4. Cook for 5 minutes and leave aside for now.
5. Drain quinoa, transfer to a bowl and add tomatoes, corn, coriander, onions, chili, lime zest, olive oil, and salt and black pepper to taste and toss.
6. In another bowl, mix avocado with lime juice and stir well.
7. Add this to the quinoa salad and chicken.
8. Toss to coat, and serve.

10 minutes

20 minutes

2

NUTRITION

Calories per serving: 300 ; Fats: 16.5g; Protein: 12.5g ; Carbohydrates: 36g

VEGGIE COMBO

15 minutes

25 minutes

4

INGREDIENTS

- 1 tablespoon of olive oil
- 1 small yellow onion, chopped
- 1 teaspoon of fresh thyme, chopped
- 1 garlic clove, minced
- 8 ounces of fresh button mushroom, sliced
- 1 pound of Brussels sprouts
- 3 cups of fresh spinach
- 4 tablespoons of walnuts
- Salt and ground black pepper, to taste

DIRECTIONS

1. In a large skillet, heat the oil over a medium heat and sauté the onion for about 3-4 minutes.
2. Add the thyme and garlic and sauté for about 1 minute.
3. Add the mushrooms and cook for about 15 minutes, or until caramelized.
4. Add the Brussels sprouts and cook for about 2-3 minutes.
5. Stir in the spinach and cook for about 3-4 minutes.
6. Stir in the walnuts, salt, and black pepper, and remove from the heat.
7. Serve hot.

NUTRITION

Calories per serving: 87 ; Fats: 3.5g ; Carbohydrates: 16g ; Protein: 5.7g

CAULIFLOWER ZUCCHINI FRITTERS

15 minutes

10 minutes

4

INGREDIENTS

- 3 cups of cauliflower florets
- ¼ tsp of black pepper
- ¼ cup of coconut flour
- 2 medium zucchinis, grated and squeezed
- 1 tbsp of coconut oil
- ½ tsp of sea salt

DIRECTIONS

1. Steam cauliflower florets for 5 minutes.
2. Place them in the food processor and process until it looks like rice.
3. Add all ingredients, except for the coconut oil, to the large bowl and mix until well combined. Make small round patties from the mixture and set them aside.
4. Heat coconut oil in a pan over a medium heat. Place patties in a pan and cook for 3-4 minutes on each side. Serve and enjoy.

NUTRITION

Calories per serving: 75; Fats: 2.2g; Carbohydrates: 10g; Protein: 3g

BEET SOUP

INGREDIENTS

- 2 cups of coconut yogurt
- 4 teaspoons of fresh lemon juice
- 2 cups of beets, trimmed, peeled, and chopped
- 2 tablespoons of fresh dill
- Salt, to taste
- 1 tablespoon of pumpkin seeds
- 2 tablespoons of coconut cream
- 1 tablespoon of fresh chives, minced

DIRECTIONS

1. In a high-speed blender, add all ingredients and pulse until smooth.
2. Transfer the soup into a pan over medium heat and cook for about 3–5 minutes or until heated through.
3. Serve immediately with a garnish of chives and coconut cream.

10 minutes

5 minutes

2

NUTRITION

Calories per serving: 128 ; Fats: 4g ; Carbohydrates: 21g ; Protein: 10g

TOFU WITH BRUSSELS SPROUTS

INGREDIENTS

- 5 tablespoons of olive oil
- 8 ounces of extra-firm tofu, drained, pressed, and cut into slices
- 2 garlic cloves, chopped
- 1/3 cup pecans, toasted, and chopped
- 1 tablespoon unsweetened applesauce
- 1/4 cup fresh cilantro, chopped
- 1/2 pound Brussels sprouts, trimmed and cut into wide ribbons
- 3/4 pound mixed bell peppers, seeded and sliced

DIRECTIONS

1. In a skillet, heat a 1/2 tablespoon of the oil over a medium heat and sauté the tofu for about 6–7 minutes, or until golden-brown.
2. Add the garlic and pecans and sauté for about 1 minute.
3. Add the applesauce and cook for about 2 minutes.
4. Stir in the cilantro and remove from the heat.
5. Transfer the tofu onto a plate and set aside
6. In the same skillet, heat the remaining oil over a medium-high heat and cook the Brussels sprouts and bell peppers for about 5 minutes.
7. Stir in the tofu and remove from the heat.
8. Serve immediately.

15 minutes

15 minutes

3

NUTRITION

Calories per serving: 365 ; Fats: 30g ; Carbohydrates: 11.5g ; Protein: 11g

COCONUT GRATIN

10 minutes

50 minutes

8

INGREDIENTS

- 3 tablespoons of olive oil
- 3 garlic cloves, minced
- 1 tablespoon of balsamic vinegar
- 1/3 cup of coconut cream
- A pinch of salt and black pepper
- 2 tablespoons of marjoram, chopped
- ½ cup of parmesan, grated
- 3 pounds of tomatoes, sliced
- Cooking spray

DIRECTIONS

1. Heat up a pan with the olive oil over a medium heat
2. Add the garlic, stir and cook for 2 minutes.
3. Add the vinegar, coconut cream, salt, pepper and marjoram, stir and cook for 3 minutes more.
4. Grease a baking dish with cooking spray and arrange the tomato slices.
5. Pour the coconut cream, mix all over, spread and sprinkle parmesan on top.
6. Place it in the oven and bake at 400 degrees F for 45 minutes.
7. Divide the gratin between plates and serve as a side dish.

NUTRITION

Calories per serving: 70; Fats: 4g; Carbohydrates: 7g; Protein: 4

AVOCADO AND WATERMELON MIX

10 minutes

0 minutes

4

INGREDIENTS

- 1½ cups of chopped tomatoes
- 1½ cups watermelon, cubed
- ½ jalapeno, chopped
- A pinch of salt and black pepper
- 1 avocado, peeled, pitted and cubed
- ½ teaspoon olive oil
- 2 tablespoons of ginger, grated
- Zest of 1 lime, grated
- 2 teaspoons of black sesame seeds
- 2 tablespoons of mint, chopped
- 3 tablespoons of lime juice

DIRECTIONS

1. In a salad bowl, combine the tomatoes with the watermelon, jalapeno, salt, pepper, avocado, oil, ginger, lime zest, black seeds, mint and lime juice.
2. Toss, divide between plates and serve as a side dish.

NUTRITION

Calories per serving: 80; Fats: 5g; Carbohydrates: 8g; Protein: 2.2g

CELERY AND CHILI PEPPERS STIR FRY

INGREDIENTS

- 2 tablespoons of olive oil
- 3 chili peppers, dried and crushed
- 4 cups of julienned celery
- 2 tablespoons of coconut aminos

DIRECTIONS

1. Heat up a pan with the oil at medium-high heat, add chili peppers, stir and cook them for 2 minutes.
2. Add the celery and the coconut aminos, stir and cook for 3 minutes more.
3. Divide between plates and serve as a side dish.

NUTRITION

Calories per serving: 42; Fats: 2g; Carbohydrates: 7.2g; Protein: 1.5g

10 minutes

5 minutes

6

THYME MUSHROOMS

INGREDIENTS

- 1 tbsp of chopped thyme
- 2 tbsps of olive oil
- 2 tbsps of chopped parsley
- 4 garlic cloves, minced
- 1 tbps of black pepper
- 2 lbs of halved white mushrooms

DIRECTIONS

1. Pre-heat your oven at 400F
2. In a baking pan, combine the mushrooms with the garlic and the other ingredients and toss,
3. Place in the oven and cook for 30 minutes.
4. Divide between plates and serve.

NUTRITION

Calories per serving: 116; Fats: 7.5g; Carbohydrates: 9g ; Protein: 7.5g

10 minutes

30 minutes

4

PESTO GREEN BEANS

10 minutes

15 minutes

4

INGREDIENTS

- 2 tbsps of olive oil
- 2 tsps of sweet paprika
- Juice of 1 lemon
- 2 tbsps of basil pesto
- 1 lb of trimmed and halved green beans
- 1/4 tsp of black pepper
- 1 sliced red onion

DIRECTIONS

1. Heat the oil in a pan over a medium heat
2. Add the onions, stir and fry for 5 minutes.
3. Add the beans and the rest of the ingredients.
4. Toss and cook over a medium heat for 10 minutes.
5. Divide between plates and serve.

NUTRITION

Calories per serving: 115 ; Fats: 6.5g ; Carbohydrates: 11g ; Protein: 3g

CAULIFLOWER MASHED "POTATOES"

10 minutes

10 minutes

4

INGREDIENTS

- 16 cups of water (enough to cover the cauliflower)
- 1 head of cauliflower (about 3 pounds), trimmed and cut into florets
- 4 garlic cloves
- 1 tablespoon of olive oil
- 1/4 teaspoon of salt
- 1/8 teaspoon of freshly ground black pepper
- 2 teaspoons of dried parsley

DIRECTIONS

1. Boil the water and then add the cauliflower and garlic.
2. Cook for about 10 minutes or until the cauliflower is fork tender.
3. Drain and return it back to the hot pan, letting it stand for 2 to 3 minutes with the lid on.
4. Transfer the cauliflower and garlic to a food processor or blender. Add the olive oil, salt, pepper, and purée until smooth.
5. Taste and adjust the salt and pepper. Remove to a serving bowl, add the parsley, and mix until combined.
6. Garnish with additional olive oil, if desired. Serve immediately.
7. Ingredient tip: if you don't have a food processor or blender, you can make this dish just as you would make mashed potatoes by using a potato masher or hand blender.

NUTRITION

Calories per serving: 44 ; Fats: 0.25g; Carbohydrate: 7.5g; Protein: 4g

ROASTED BRUSSELS SPROUTS

INGREDIENTS

- 1½ pounds Brussels sprouts, trimmed and halved
- 2 tablespoons olive oil
- ¼ teaspoon salt
- ½ teaspoon freshly ground black pepper

DIRECTIONS

Preheat the oven to 400°f.

1. Combine the Brussels sprouts and olive oil in a large mixing bowl and toss until they are evenly coated.
2. Turn the Brussels sprouts out onto a large baking sheet and flip them over so they are cut-side down with the flat part touching the baking sheet. Sprinkle with salt and pepper.
3. Bake for 20 to 30 minutes or until the Brussels sprouts are lightly charred, crispy on the outside and toasted on the bottom. The outer leaves will be extra dark, too.
4. Serve immediately.

5 minutes

20 minutes

4

Ingredient tip when choosing Brussels sprouts: look for bright-green heads that are firm and heavy for their size. The leaves should be tightly packed. Avoid sprouts with yellowing leaves—a sign of age—or black spots—which means they could have fungus.

NUTRITION

Calories per serving: 106; Fats: 7g ; Carbohydrate: 11g; Protein: 4g

---

BROCCOLI WITH GARLIC AND LEMON

INGREDIENTS

- 1 cup of water
- 4 cups of broccoli florets
- 1 teaspoon of olive oil
- 1 tablespoon of minced garlic
- 1 teaspoon of lemon zest
- Salt
- Freshly ground black pepper

DIRECTIONS

1. In a small saucepan, bring 1 cup of water to a boil.
2. Add the broccoli to the boiling water and cook for 2 to 3 minutes or until tender, being careful not to overcook. The broccoli should retain its bright-green color.
3. Drain the water from the broccoli.
4. In a small sauté pan over medium-high heat, add the olive oil. Add the garlic and sauté for 30 seconds. Add the broccoli, lemon zest, salt, and pepper. Combine well and serve.

2 minutes

4 minutes

4

Ingredient tip: to retain the most nutrients in your vegetables, it is important not to overcook them, as the vitamins and minerals will leach out into the cooking water. Steamer baskets are inexpensive and are a good way to quickly cook veggies. Another way to minimize nutrient loss is to steam in the microwave by adding the vegetables to a microwave-safe dish with a couple of tablespoons of water and cooking on high for 2 to 3 minutes.

NUTRITION

Calories per serving: 32; Fats: 0.25g ; Carbohydrate: 7.5g; Protein: 3g

123

5 minutes

10 minutes

4

BROWN-RICE PILAF

INGREDIENTS

- 1 cup of low-sodium vegetable broth
- ½ tablespoon of olive oil
- 1 clove of garlic, minced
- 1 scallion, thinly sliced
- 1 tablespoon of minced onion flakes
- 1 cup of instant brown rice
- 1/8 teaspoon of freshly ground black pepper

DIRECTIONS

1. Mix the vegetable broth, olive oil, garlic, scallion, and minced onion flakes in a saucepan and bring to a boil.
2. Add rice, return mixture to the boil, then reduce the heat and simmer for 10 minutes.
3. Remove from heat and let it stand for 5 minutes.
4. Fluff with a fork and season with black pepper.

Ingredient tip: the nutritional differences between a serving of long-grain brown rice, which requires 35 to 45 minutes to cook, and instant brown rice, which cooks in about 10 minutes, is insignificant. Instant rice has simply been cooked and dehydrated so it cooks quicker than long-grain rice. Feel free to use both varieties.

NUTRITION

Calories per serving: 75; Fats: 3.5g; Carbohydrate: 10g; Protein: 1.5g

MASHED CAULIFLOWER

INGREDIENTS

- 1 cauliflower head
- 1 tablespoon of olive oil
- ½ tsp of salt
- ¼ tsp of dill
- Pepper to taste
- 2 tbsp. low-fat milk

DIRECTIONS

1. Place a small pot of water to boil.
2. Chop the cauliflower into florets.
3. Add florets to the boiling water and boil uncovered for 5 minutes. Turn off the heat and let it sit for 5 minutes more.
4. In a blender, add all the ingredients except for the cauliflower and blend to mix well.
5. Drain the cauliflower well and add it to a blender. Puree until smooth and creamy.
6. Serve and enjoy.

10 minutes

10 minutes

NUTRITION

Calories per serving: 45 ; Fats: 3g ; Carbohydrates: 7g ; Protein: 4g

3

SAUTÉED GARLIC MUSHROOMS

10 minutes

10 minutes

4

INGREDIENTS

- 1 tablespoon of olive oil
- 3 cloves of garlic, minced
- 16 ounces of fresh brown mushrooms, sliced
- 7 ounces of fresh shiitake mushrooms, sliced
- ½ tsp of salt
- ½ tsp of pepper or more to taste

DIRECTIONS

1. Place a nonstick saucepan on medium-high heat and it for a minute.
2. Add oil and heat for 2 minutes.
3. Stir in the garlic and sauté for a minute.
4. Add the remaining ingredients and stir fry until soft and tender, for around 5 minutes.
5. Turn off the heat and let the mushrooms rest while the pan is covered for 5 minutes.
6. Serve and enjoy.

NUTRITION

Calories per serving: 44; Fats: 3.5g; Carbohydrates: 2g; Protein 2.2g

CASHEW PESTO & PARSLEY WITH VEGGIES

15 minutes

10 minutes

3-4

INGREDIENTS

- 3 zucchini (sliced)
- 8 bamboo skewers, soaked in water
- 2 red capsicums
- ¼ cup olive oil
- 750 grams Eggplant
- 4 lemon wedges
- For Serving:
- 1 cup of couscous salad
- Preparing the cashew pesto:
- ½ cup of cashew (roasted)
- ½ cup of parsley
- 2 cup of grated parmesan
- 2 tbsp of lime juice
- ¼ cup of olive oil

DIRECTIONS

1. Toss the capsicum, eggplant, and zucchini with oil and salt and thread it onto the skewers.
2. Cook the bamboo sticks for 6-8 minutes on a barbecue grill pan on a medium heat.
3. Also, grill the lemon wedges on both sides.
4. For preparing the cashew pesto, combine all of the ingredients in the food processor and blend.
5. For serving, place the grill skewers on a plate with the grilled lemon slices and drizzle some cashew pesto over the top.

NUTRITION

Calories per serving: 352; Protein: 25g; Fats: 22g ; Carbohydrates: 20g

SPICY CHICKPEAS WITH ROASTED VEGETABLES

INGREDIENTS

- 1 large carrot (peeled)
- 2tbsp of sunflower oil
- 1 head of cauliflower
- 1tbsp of ground cumin
- ½ a red onion, diced
- 1 red pepper, deseeded
- 400g can of chickpeas

DIRECTIONS

1. Preheat the oven to 430F
2. Cut all the vegetables and toss with salt, pepper and onion.
3. In a bowl, whisk the olive oil, pepper, and cumin powder.
4. Add all veggies to the bowl and toss.
5. Transfer the vegetables onto a lined baking tin and bake for almost 15 minutes.
6. Now add chickpeas and stir.
7. Return to the oven and bake for 10 minutes.
8. Serve it with toast or bread.

10 minutes

25 minutes

2-3

NUTRITION

Calories per serving: 488; Protein: 24g; Fats: 13g ; Carbohydrates: 74g

TURMERIC PEPPERS PLATTER

INGREDIENTS

- 2 green bell peppers, cut into wedges
- 2 red bell peppers, cut into wedges
- 2 yellow bell peppers, cut into wedges
- 2 tablespoons of avocado oil
- 2 garlic cloves, minced
- 1 bunch of basil, chopped
- A pinch of salt and black pepper
- 2 tablespoons of balsamic vinegar

DIRECTIONS

1. Heat a pan with the oil on medium heat, add the garlic and the vinegar and cook for 2 minutes.
2. Add the peppers and the other ingredients, toss, cook over medium heat for 18 minutes, arrange them on a platter and serve as an appetizer.

10 minutes

20 minutes

4

NUTRITION

Calories per serving: 404; Fat 7.5g; Carbohydrates: 9.5g; Protein: 1.75

129

10 minutes

12 minutes

6

MUSHROOM CAKES

INGREDIENTS

- 1 cup of chopped shallots
- 2 tablespoons of olive oil
- 3 garlic cloves, minced
- 1 pound mushrooms, minced
- 2 tablespoons almond flour
- ¼ cup coconut cream
- 1 tablespoon flaxseed with 2 tablespoons of water
- ¼ cup of parsley, chopped

DIRECTIONS

1. In a bowl, combine the shallots with the garlic, the mushrooms, and the other ingredients except for the oil.
2. Stir well and then shape the mix into medium sized 'cakes'.
3. Heat the oil in a pan over a medium heat.
4. Add the mushroom cakes and cook for 6 minutes on each side, arranging them on a platter.
5. Serve as an appetizer.

NUTRITION

Calories per serving: 120; Fats: 6g; Carbohydrates: 8g; Protein: 6g

CABBAGE STICKS

INGREDIENTS

- 1 pound cabbage, leaves separated and cut into thick strips
- 1 tablespoon olive oil
- 1 tablespoon balsamic vinegar
- 1 teaspoon ginger, grated
- 1 teaspoon hot paprika
- A pinch of salt and black pepper

DIRECTIONS

1. Spread the cabbage strips on a baking sheet lined with parchment paper.
2. Add the oil, the vinegar, and the other ingredients, toss and cook at 400 degrees F for 30 minutes.
3. Divide the cabbage strips into bowls and serve as a snack.

NUTRITION

Calories per serving: 75; Fats: 3.5g; Carbohydrates: 6.5g; Protein: 1.5g

10 minutes

30 minutes

4

Chapter 7
Desserts and Smoothie Recipes

CINNAMON QUINOA BARS

20 minutes

30 minutes

4

INGREDIENTS

- 2 ½ cups cooked quinoa
- 4 large eggs
- 1/3 cup unsweetened almond milk
- 1/3 cup pure maple syrup
- Seeds from ½ whole vanilla bean pod or 1 tbsp vanilla extract
- 1 ½ tbsp cinnamon
- 1/4 tsp salt

DIRECTIONS

1. Preheat oven to 375oF.
2. Combine all ingredients in a large bowl and mix well.
3. In an 8 x 8 baking pan, cover with parchment paper.
4. Pour the batter evenly into a baking dish.
5. Bake for 25-30 minutes or until it has set. It should not wiggle when you lightly shake. You want the eggs to be fully cooked.
6. Remove as quickly as possible from the pan and parchment paper and place it on a cooling rack.
7. Cut into 4 pieces.
8. Enjoy on its own, with a small spread of almond or nut butter or wait until it cools to enjoy the next morning.

NUTRITION

Calories per serving: 253; Carbohydrates: 38g ; Protein: 11g ; Fats: 7g

APPLE COUSCOUS PUDDING

10 minutes

25 minutes

4

INGREDIENTS

- ½ cup couscous
- ½ cup milk
- ¼ cup of apple, cored and chopped
- 2 tbsps. stevia
- ½ tsp. rose water
- 1 tbsp. orange zest, grated

DIRECTIONS

1. Heat the milk in a pan over medium heat, add the couscous and the rest of the ingredients, whisk, simmer for 25 minutes, divide into bowls and serve.

NUTRITION

Calories 209; Fats: 1.1g; Carbohydrates: 17g; Protein: 2g

RUBY PEARS DELIGHT

INGREDIENTS

- 4 Pears
- Grape juice-26 oz.
- Currant jelly-11 oz.
- 4 garlic cloves
- Juice and zest of 1 lemon
- 4 peppercorns
- 2 rosemary springs
- 1/2 vanilla bean

DIRECTIONS

1. Pour the jelly and grape juice into a pressure cooker and mix with lemon zest and juice
2. Dip each pear in the mixture. Next and wrap them in clean tin foil and place them neatly in the steamer basket of the pressure
3. Mix peppercorns, rosemary, garlic cloves and vanilla beans with the juice mixture,
4. Seal the lid and cook on 'high' for 10 minutes.
5. Release the pressure quickly, and carefully open the lid; bring out the pears, remove skins and arrange them on plates. Serve when cold with spoonfuls of cooking juice on top.

10 minutes

10 minutes

4

NUTRITION

Calories per serving: 500 ; Fats: 1.4g ; Carbohydrates: 75g ; Protein: 2.2g

MIXED BERRY AND ORANGE COMPOTE

134

INGREDIENTS

- 1/2-pound strawberries
- 1 tablespoon orange juice
- 1/4 teaspoon ground cloves
- 1/2 cup brown sugar
- 1 vanilla bean
- 1-pound blueberries
- 1/2-pound blackberries

DIRECTIONS

1. Place your berries in the inner pot. Add the sugar and let sit for 15 minutes.
2. Add the orange juice, ground cloves, and vanilla bean.
3. Secure the lid. Choose the "Manual" mode and cook for 2 minutes at High pressure. Once cooking is complete, use a natural pressure release for 10 minutes; carefully remove the lid.
4. As your compote cools, it will thicken.

15 minutes

15 minutes

4

As a serving idea - it is great served with natural yoghurt

NUTRITION

Calories 212; Fat 0.75g; Carbohydrates 14g; Protein 2.2g

COOKIE DOUGH BITES

10 Minutes

5 Minutes

2

INGREDIENTS

- ¼ cup almond flour
- 1 ½ cups chickpeas, cooked
- ½ tsp. salt
- ½ cup almond butter or any nut butter
- ¼ cup chocolate chips, dairy-free & sugar-free
- 1 tsp. vanilla extract
- 2 tbsp. maple syrup

DIRECTIONS

1. First, place all the ingredients excluding the chocolate chips in a high-speed blender for 3 minutes or until you get a thick, smooth mixture.
2. Next, transfer the mixture into a medium-sized bowl.
3. Then, fold the chocolate chips into the batter.
4. Check for sweetness and add more maple syrup if needed.
5. Serve and enjoy.
6. Tip: Instead of maple syrup, you can also use Medjool dates.

NUTRITION

Calories per serving: 945 ; Protein: 36g ; Carbohydrates: 100g ; Fats: 45g

GREEN TEA PUDDING

20 minutes

10 minutes

3

INGREDIENTS

- 1 Tsp. Matcha Green Tea Powder
- 3 eggs
- 50g butter
- 2 cup of full milk
- Salt
- 1/4 cup brown sugar
- 1/4 cup corn starch
- 1/8-tbsp. cinnamon powder

DIRECTIONS

1. In a big pot, mix brown sugar, milk, cornstarch, and matcha powder.
2. On a medium heat, keep whisking until mixed.
3. Slowly, mix the hot batter with whisked eggs.
4. Cook for 3-5 minutes.
5. Strain the mixture and add butter.
6. Put the mixture in a container, refrigerate for a few hours and serve.

NUTRITION

Calories per serving: 588; Carbohydrates: 0.3g; Fats: 54g; Protein: 6g

ZINGY BLUEBERRY SAUCE

INGREDIENTS

- 1/4 cup of fresh lemon juice
- 1-pound of granulated sugar
- 1 tablespoon of freshly grated lemon zest
- 1/2 teaspoon of vanilla extract
- 2 pounds of fresh blueberries

DIRECTIONS

1. Place the blueberries, sugar and vanilla in the inner pot of the pressure cooker.
2. Secure the lid. Choose the "Manual" mode and cook for 2 minutes at high pressure.
3. Once cooking is complete, use a natural pressure release for 15 minutes then carefully remove the lid.
4. Stir in the lemon zest and juice.
5. Puree in a food processor then strain and push the mixture through a sieve before storing. Enjoy!

Tip: Great with natural yoghurt!

NUTRITION

Calories per serving: 227; Fat: 0.4g; Carbohydrates: 58g; Protein: 0,7g

5 minutes

20 minutes

10

10 minutes

15 minutes

3

CHOCOLATE ALMOND CUSTARD

INGREDIENTS

- 3 chocolate cookies, broken into chunks
- A pinch of salt
- 1/4 teaspoon ground cardamom
- 3 tablespoons honey
- 1/4 teaspoon freshly grated nutmeg
- 2 tablespoons butter
- 3 tablespoons whole milk
- 1 cup almond flour
- 3 eggs
- 1 teaspoon of pure vanilla extract

DIRECTIONS

1. In a mixing bowl, beat the eggs with butter. Now, add the milk and continue mixing until well combined.
2. Add the remaining ingredients in the order listed above. Divide the batter between 3 ramekins.
3. Add 1 cup of water and a metal trivet to the pressure cooker. Cover ramekins with foil and lower them onto the trivet.
4. Secure the lid and select "Manual" mode. Cook at High pressure for 12 minutes. Once cooking is complete, use a quick release; carefully remove the lid.
5. Transfer the ramekins to a wire rack and allow them to cool slightly before serving. Enjoy!

NUTRITION

Calories per serving: 402; Fat: 32g; Carbohydrates: 28g; Protein: 16g

HONEY STEWED APPLES

INGREDIENTS

- 2 tablespoons honey
- 1 teaspoon ground cinnamon
- 1/2 teaspoon ground cloves
- 4 apples

DIRECTIONS

1. Add all ingredients to the inner pot then add 1/3 cup of water.
2. Secure the lid. Choose the "Manual" mode and cook for 2 minutes at High pressure. Once cooking is complete, use a quick pressure release; carefully remove the lid.
3. Serve in individual bowls. Bon appétit!

NUTRITION

Calories per serving: 113; Fat: 0.3g; Carbohydrates: 32g; Protein: 0.7g

5 minutes

5 minutes

4

VANILLA BREAD PUDDING WITH APRICOTS

INGREDIENTS

- 2 tablespoons coconut oil
- 1 1/3 cups heavy cream
- 4 eggs, whisked
- 1/2 cup dried apricots, soaked and then chopped
- 1 teaspoon cinnamon, ground
- 1/2 teaspoon star anise, ground
- A pinch of grated nutmeg
- A pinch of salt
- 1/2 cup granulated sugar
- 2 tablespoons molasses
- 2 cups of milk
- 4 cups of Italian bread, cubed
- 1 teaspoon of vanilla paste

DIRECTIONS

1. Add 1 ½ cups of water and a metal rack to the pressure cooker.
2. Grease a baking dish with a nonstick cooking spray. Throw the bread cubes into the prepared baking dish.
3. In a mixing bowl, thoroughly combine the remaining ingredients. Pour the mixture over the bread cubes. Cover with a piece of foil, making a foil sling.
4. Secure the lid. Choose the "Porridge" mode and High pressure; cook for 15 minutes. Once cooking is complete, use a quick pressure release; carefully remove the lid. Enjoy!

NUTRITION

Calories per serving: 200; Fats: 11.5g; Carbohydrates 6g; Protein 19g

5 minutes

15 minutes

6

MEDITERRANEAN-STYLE CARROT PUDDING

15 minutes

15 minutes

4

INGREDIENTS

- 1/3 cup almonds, ground
- 1/4 cup dried figs, chopped
- 2 large-sized carrots, grated
- 1/2 cup water
- 1 ½ cups milk
- 1/2 teaspoon ground star anise
- 1/3 teaspoon ground cardamom
- 1/4 teaspoon kosher salt
- 2 tbps granulated sugar
- 2 eggs, beaten
- 1/2 teaspoon pure almond extract
- 1/2 teaspoon vanilla extract
- 1 ½ cups jasmine rice

DIRECTIONS

1. Place the jasmine rice, milk, water, carrots, and salt in the pressure cooker.
2. Stir to combine and secure the lid. Choose "Manual" and cook at High pressure for 10 minutes. Once cooking is complete, use a natural release for 15 minutes; carefully remove the lid.
3. Now, press the "Sauté" button and add the sugar, eggs, and almonds; stir to combine well. Bring to a boil; press the "Keep Heat/ Cancel" button.
4. Add the remaining ingredients and stir; the pudding will thicken as it sits. Bon appétit!

NUTRITION

Calories per serving: 220; Fat: 9.5g; Carbohydrates: 26.5g; Protein: 9g

---

CHOCOLATE RICE

10 minutes

20 minutes

4

INGREDIENTS

- 1 cup of rice
- 1 tbsp cocoa powder
- 2 tbsp maple syrup
- 2 cups almond milk

DIRECTIONS

1. Add all the ingredients to the inner pot of a pressure cooker and stir well.
2. Seal the pot with its lid and cook on high for 20 minutes.
3. Once done, allow the pressure to release naturally for 10 minutes then release the remaining using quick release. Remove the lid.
4. Stir and serve.

NUTRITION

Calories per serving: 70; Fats: 2.5g ; Carbohydrates: 14 g ; Protein: 2g

RAISINS WITH CINNAMON AND PEACHES

INGREDIENTS

- 4 peaches, cored and cut into chunks
- 1 tsp vanilla
- 1 tsp cinnamon
- 1/2 cup raisins
- 1 cup of water

DIRECTIONS

1. Add all the ingredients to the inner pot of a pressure cooker and stir well.
2. Seal the pot with a lid and cook on high for 15 minutes.
3. Once done, allow the pressure to release naturally for 10 minutes then release the remaining pressure using quick release. Remove the lid.
4. Stir and serve.

NUTRITION

Calories per serving: 122 ; Fats: 0.5g ; Carbohydrates: 30g; Protein: 2g

10 minutes

15 minutes

4

LEMON PEAR COMPOTE

INGREDIENTS

- 3 cups pears, cored and cut into chunks
- 1 tsp vanilla
- 1 tsp liquid stevia
- 1 tbsp lemon zest, grated
- 2 tbsp lemon juice

DIRECTIONS

1. Add all ingredients to the inner pot of a pressure cooker and stir well.
2. Seal the pot with a lid and cook on high for 15 minutes.
3. Once done, allow the pressure to release naturally for 10 minutes then release the remaining pressure using quick release. Remove the lid.
4. Stir and serve.

NUTRITION

Calories per serving: 40; Fats: 0.2g ; Carbohydrates: 16g; Protein: 0.5g

10 minutes

15 minutes

6

145

4 minutes

0 minutes

2

MINTY COCONUT CREAM

INGREDIENTS

- 1 banana, peeled
- 2 cups coconut flesh, shredded
- 3 tablespoons mint, chopped
- 1 and ½ cups coconut water
- 2 tablespoons stevia
- ½ avocado, pitted and peeled

DIRECTIONS

1. In a blender, combine the coconut with the banana and the rest of the ingredients, pulse well, divide into cups and serve cold.

NUTRITION

Calories per serving: 421 ; Fats: 36g ; Carbohydrates: 26g ; Protein: 4g

FRESH FRUIT SMOOTHIE

INGREDIENTS

- ½ cup chopped fresh pineapple
- ½ cup chopped fresh strawberries
- ¼ cup cantaloupe or other melon, peeled, deseeded, chopped
- Juice of 1 orange
- ½ tablespoon honey
- ½ cup water

DIRECTIONS

1. Combine pineapple, strawberries, cantaloupe, orange juice, honey, and water in a blender. Blitz until you get smooth puree.
2. Pour into 2 tall glasses and serve with crushed ice immediately.

10 minutes

0 minutes

2

NUTRITION

Calories per serving: 75; Fats: 0 ; Carbohydrate: 18g ; Protein: 1.5g

ORANGE DREAM SMOOTHIE

5 minutes

0 minutes

2

INGREDIENTS

- ¾ cup chilled orange juice
- 3 tablespoons silken or soft tofu
- ½ teaspoon grated orange zest
- Ice cubes, as required
- ½ cup light vanilla soymilk, chilled
- ½ tablespoon dark honey
- ¼ teaspoon vanilla extract
- 2 orange slices to garnish

DIRECTIONS

1. Place orange juice, tofu, orange zest, ice cubes, soymilk, honey, and vanilla into the blender jar.
2. Blitz until you get a smooth puree.
3. Pour into 2 tall glasses.
4. Garnish with an orange slice in each glass and serve.

NUTRITION

Calories per serving: 150; Fats: 1g; Total Carbohydrate: 33g; Protein: 2.5g

CHOCOLATE PUDDING SMOOTHIE

5 minutes

0 minutes

1

INGREDIENTS

- 1 cup vanilla soymilk
- ½ a medium banana, chopped
- ¼ avocado, pitted, peeled, chopped
- 1 packet splenda or stevia
- 2 tablespoons unsweetened cocoa powder

DIRECTIONS

1. Blitz together soymilk, bananas, avocado, splenda, and cocoa powder in a blender until you get a smooth puree.
2. Pour into a tall glass and serve with ice if desired.

NUTRITION

Calories per serving: 305; Fats: 12g ; Carbohydrate: 57g ; Protein: 12g

ALMOND SMOOTHIE

INGREDIENTS

- ¾ cup almonds, chopped
- ½ cup heavy whipping cream
- 2 teaspoons butter, melted
- ¼ teaspoon organic vanilla extract
- 7–8 drops liquid stevia
- 1 cup unsweetened almond milk
- ¼ cup ice cubes

DIRECTIONS

1. In a blender, put all the listed ingredients and pulse until creamy.
2. Pour the smoothie into two glasses and serve immediately.

10 minutes

10 minutes

NUTRITION

Calories per serving: 539; Carbohydrates: 13g ; Fats: 49g ; Protein: 13g

2

MOCHA SMOOTHIE

INGREDIENTS

- 2 teaspoons instant espresso powder
- 2–3 tablespoons granulated erythritol
- 2 teaspoons cacao powder
- ½ cup plain Greek yogurt
- 1cupunsweetened almond milk
- 1 cup ice cubes

DIRECTIONS

1. In a blender, put all the listed ingredients and pulse until creamy.
2. Pour the smoothie into two glasses and serve immediately.

10 minutes

10 minutes

NUTRITION

Calories per serving: 65; Carbohydrates: 8.5g ; Fats: 2g ; Protein: 4g

2

Chapter 8
21 Days Meal Plan

DAY	BREAKFAST (PREPARE SOME IN ADVANCE)	LUNCH	DINNER
1	MOCHA SMOOTHIE	Chicken, barley and leek stew	Salmon Wrap
2	CINNAMON QUINOA BARS	Barley with Lentils, Mushrooms, and Tahini-Yogurt Sauce	Baked Fish Served with Vegetables
3	APPLE COUSCOUS PUDDING	Garlic Shrimp Fettuccine	Turkey and Cranberry Sauce
4	RUBY PEARS DELIGHT	Kale White Bean Soup	Green Goddess Crab Salad with Endive
5	CHOCOLATE PUDDING SMOOTHIE	Garlic and Parsley Chickpeas	Seared Scallops with Blood Orange Glaze
6	MIXED BERRY AND ORANGE COMPOTE	Beef with Mushroom and Broccoli	Grilled Mahi-Mahi with Artichoke Caponata
7	COOKIE DOUGH BITES	Greek Chickpeas with Coriander and Sage	Lemon Garlic Shrimp
8	ORANGE DREAM SMOOTHIE	Creamy chicken noodle soup	Lemon Salmon with Kaffir Lime
9	GREEN TEA PUDDING	Spiced Ground Beef	Sardine Bruschetta with Fennel and Lemon Crema

10	ZINGY BLUEBERRY SAUCE	French Lentils with Carrots and Parsley	Fish in A Vegetable Patch
11	CHOCOLATE ALMOND CUSTARD	Chickpeas with Garlic and Parsley	Hearty Lemon and Pepper Chicken
12	HONEY STEWED APPLES	Chopped Tuna Salad	Ground Beef with Veggies
13	VANILLA BREAD PUDDING WITH APRICOTS	Roasted Ratatouille Pasta	Roasted Chicken Thighs
14	MEDITERRANEAN-STYLE CARROT PUDDING	Spicy Chickpeas with Turnips	Lemon Garlic Chicken
15	MOCHA SMOOTHIE	Zucchini Beef Sauté with Coriander Greens	Caramelized Fennel and Sardines with Penne
16	CHOCOLATE RICE	Chickpea Salad with Carrots, Arugula, and Olives	Turkey With Basil & Tomatoes
17	RAISINS WITH CINNAMON AND PEACHES	Beef Soup	Flounder with Tomatoes and Basil
18	ALMOND SMOOTHIE	Quick Shrimp Fettuccine	Chicken and tzatziki pitas
19	LEMON PEAR COMPOTE	Spicy mustard chicken	Cod and Cauliflower Chowder
20	MINTY COCONUT CREAM	Lentil and Mushroom Pasta	Chicken with Potatoes Olives & Sprouts
21	FRESH FRUIT SMOOTHIE	Ground Beef with Greens and Tomatoes	Monkfish with Sautéed Leeks, Fennel, and Tomatoes

DISCOVER THE AMAZING BONUS I HAVE IN STORE FOR YOU

Scan the QR Code or go to www.vitaminsmineralsguides.com
for instant access to the 2 FREE life-saving guides that come with this Book:

FREE: A PRACTICAL 70+ PAGE GUIDEBOOK

Discover the vitamins and minerals that should never be missing from your diet - and which foods you can get them from-.

A free ultra-detailed report – suitable for beginners too – to discover all the essential nutrients for living a long and healthy life.

Here is everything you will find in this guide:

» What are vitamins and why are they essential

» Minerals - what they do and why you should never be missing them in your diet-

» The 8 signs that you are deficient in vitamins or minerals and how to remedy that

» 3 facts that (maybe) you won't know about vitamins and minerals

» And much much more...

Printed in Great Britain
by Amazon

10082499R00072